What's Next?

Monthly Extensions to **Challenge Proficient Students** in a PLC at Work®

MARK WEICHEL STEVE PEARCE

Solution Tree | Press

555 North Morton Street
Bloomington, IN 47404
800.733.6786 (toll free) / 812.336.7700
FAX: 812.336.7790

email: info@SolutionTree.com
SolutionTree.com

Visit **go.SolutionTree.com/PLCbooks** to download the free reproducibles in this book.

Printed in the United States of America

Library of Congress Cataloging-in-Publication Data

Names: Weichel, Mark, author.
Title: What's next? : monthly extensions to challenge proficient students in a PLC at work / Mark Weichel, Steve Pearce.
Other titles: What is next?
Description: Bloomington, IN : Solution Tree Press, [2022] | Includes bibliographical references and index.
Identifiers: LCCN 2022002838 (print) | LCCN 2022002839 (ebook) | ISBN 9781951075835 (Paperback) | ISBN 9781951075842 (eBook)
Subjects: LCSH: Professional learning communities--United States. | Teaching teams--United States. | Effective teaching--United States. | Individualized instruction--United States.
Classification: LCC LB1731 .W392 2022 (print) | LCC LB1731 (ebook) | DDC 371.14/80973--dc23/eng/20220225
LC record available at https://lccn.loc.gov/2022002838
LC ebook record available at https://lccn.loc.gov/2022002839

Solution Tree
Jeffrey C. Jones, CEO
Edmund M. Ackerman, President

Solution Tree Press
President and Publisher: Douglas M. Rife
Associate Publisher: Sarah Payne-Mills
Art Director: Rian Anderson
Managing Production Editor: Kendra Slayton
Editorial Director: Todd Brakke
Copy Chief: Jessi Finn
Production Editor: Miranda Addonizio
Content Development Specialist: Amy Rubenstein
Acquisitions Editor: Sarah Jubar
Proofreader: Evie Madsen
Text and Cover Designer: Rian Anderson
Associate Editor: Sarah Ludwig
Editorial Assistants: Charlotte Jones and Elijah Oates

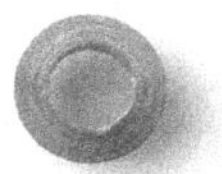

ACKNOWLEDGMENTS

Thank you to the following educators who shared their extension activities and experiences.

- Mikayla Bruner, Excellence in Youth teacher, Westside Community Schools (Nebraska)
- Holly Compton, teacher on special assignment, Manhattan Beach Unified School District (California)
- Bill Ferriter, teacher and education consultant, Wake County Public Schools (North Carolina)
- Brett Geithman, superintendent, Larkspur-Corte Madera School District (California)
- Julie Jensen, learning and innovation manager, Kinkaid Information Technology (Kansas)
- Lori Little, gifted education coordinator, Louisville Public Schools (Nebraska)
- Kristie Nelson, teacher, McKeel Academy (Florida)
- Brad Newkirk, assistant superintendent, Batavia Public Schools (Illinois)
- Julie Schonewise, English teacher, Lincoln Pius X High School (Nebraska)
- Ming Shelby, director of professional learning, Batavia Public Schools (Illinois)
- Katie Sindt, Excellence in Youth teacher, Westside Community Schools (Nebraska)

- Randy Smasal, assistant superintendent, Edina Public Schools (Minnesota)
- Todd Smith, CEO, Symphony Workforce (Nebraska)

Solution Tree Press would like to thank the following reviewers:

Chris Bennett
Principal
Burns Middle School
Lawndale, North Carolina

Rea Smith
Math Facilitator
Rogers Public Schools
Rogers, Arkansas

Jennifer Steele
Assistant Principal
Northside High School
Fort Smith, Arkansas

Dawn Vang
Assistant Principal
McDeeds Creek Elementary
Southern Pines, North Carolina

Visit **go.SolutionTree.com/PLCbooks** to download the free reproducibles in this book.

TABLE OF CONTENTS

Reproducible pages are in italics.

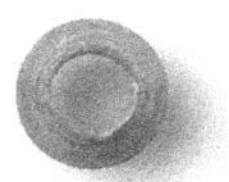

ABOUT THE AUTHORS

Mark Weichel, EdD, is assistant superintendent for teaching and learning at Westside Community Schools in Omaha, Nebraska. While he has served in this role, the district has received local and national attention for its commitment to collaboration, innovation, technology integration, and personalized learning. Mark and his team developed collaborative systems that have been written about in various journals, and they host visiting districts and regularly present at state and national conferences.

Previously, Mark was director of secondary curriculum, a high school building administrator, and a junior high school social studies teacher at Papillion La Vista Community Schools in Nebraska. He and staff implemented Professional Learning Communities at Work® strategies and failure rates plummeted while standardized testing measures such as ACT, PLAN, and state writing assessments confirmed high levels of student learning.

Mark and his leadership team at Papillion La Vista South High School presented at conferences nationwide, and their work was featured on AllThingsPLC.info and in *Principal Leadership* magazine. They received the 2008 Ethel Percy Andrus Legacy Award for Innovation from the American Association of Retired Persons (AARP). Mark also taught in the graduate schools for Peru State College and the University of Nebraska Omaha.

Mark earned a doctorate in educational administration from the University ofNebraska Omaha. To learn more about Mark's work, follow @westsideweichel on Twitter.

Steve Pearce is the chief human resources officer for Batavia Public School District 101 in Batavia, Illinois. Batavia Public School District is recognized for its innovation and dedication to a guaranteed and viable curriculum, collaboration, and personalized learning. He is former principal of Jane Addams Junior High and Margaret Mead Junior High schools, both in Schaumburg School District 54 in Illinois. During his tenure at Addams and Mead, Steve led his staffs in building professional learning communities (PLCs) with tremendous results. Steve and the staffs of Addams and Mead have assisted other educators in launching their PLC journeys by hosting interested school staffs for site visits. In addition, Steve has delivered presentations on the PLC at Work process to schools across the nation.

In his first year at Addams in 2008–2009, Steve guided the staff to the highest levels of student achievement in the school's forty-year history. Addams also achieved the 90/90 board goal for two consecutive years, where 90 percent of the students achieved meets-or-exceeds status on the state assessment in both reading and mathematics. In 2010, Addams was recognized as a top one hundred high-performing schools in Illinois for the first time in school history.

In just three years at Mead, student achievement reached the highest levels in the school's twenty-eight-year history. In 2007, Mead was recognized in the top-fifty high-performing middle schools in the Chicago suburbs for the first time. Mead received the Academic Improvement Award from the Illinois School Board of Education for standardized test score gains. After reviewing Mead's PLC implementation, PLC at Work architect Richard DuFour stated, "Mead could serve as a national model of what middle schools should be."

For all of these remarkable achievements, Addams and Mead are both featured on allthingsplc.info as evidence of effectiveness of the PLC at Work process.

To learn more about Steve's work, follow @stevepearce4 on Twitter.

To book Mark Weichel or Steve Pearce for professional development, contact pd@solutiontree.com.

INTRODUCTION

Chances are, if you have picked up this book, you have been working as a member of a collaborative team that has overcome many of the traditional obstacles to developing an effective Professional Learning Community (PLC) at Work®. You have all staff members working in teams with collaborative time reserved on a weekly basis within the workday, and your teams have worked together to develop a guaranteed and viable curriculum, offer common formative assessments, and use data protocols to guide your conversations and next steps. These conversations allow you and your team members to better ensure students learn at high levels, determine which students need more support, and have a systematic way to intervene on behalf of students who need more time and support. There are many great articles, books, and tools available to assist teams in developing these skills, including the seminal guidebook for implementing PLCs, *Learning by Doing: A Handbook for Professional Learning Communities at Work* (DuFour, DuFour, Eaker, Many, & Mattos, 2016), and www.allthingsPLC.info, the enormously useful repository of data, evidence, and research.

If you and your team are like many of the high-performing teams we have worked with in each of our more than twenty-year careers in education, another likely key feature of your experience is that you struggle with what to do with students who already excel when they enter your classroom. This struggle is one of the most common issues that teams face when dealing with the diverse needs of their students. Is this an issue or challenge for your team? If you are not a member of a collaborative team or are on a team that has yet to become high performing, this is a great opportunity to get systems in place to do the right work from day one.

Teams in the PLC at Work process, as developed by PLC architects Richard DuFour, Rebecca DuFour, and Robert Eaker, ground themselves with the four critical questions of a PLC (DuFour et al., 2016).

1. What is it we want our students to know and be able to do?
2. How will we know if each student has learned it?
3. How will we respond when some students do not learn it?
4. How will we extend the learning for students who have demonstrated proficiency?

By understanding the needs of proficient students and the strategies described in this book, teams will be equipped to better meet the needs of all students. As many teams become proficient on the first three questions before embarking on question 4, by starting out with a solid understanding of all four questions, your team will have a more complete picture before you start.

The fourth question, about what to do if students already know it, often gets forgotten for a few different reasons. In many ways, the four critical questions are linear; teachers need to accomplish one before moving on to the next. For example, it is difficult to determine what students know if you haven't determined what you want them to know. It is hard to figure out what interventions will look like before you settle on how you will know what students have learned. Often, by the time teams are ready to discuss question 4, they have run out of time and are preparing for the next unit.

Another reason is priorities. Many teachers will say that they are more worried about the students who don't already know the material. Students who know the material will be fine and will still pass the test. The last reason that teachers we work with frequently share with us is that they just don't know how. Even if they knew which students already know the material, they simply don't know what to do with them. We can help with that.

Throughout this book, we refer to students who are passionate about a subject and walk into the classroom already knowing the information you are preparing to teach as *question 4 students* for that unit or specific skill. Please note that students being passionate about a certain subject does not automatically mean they should continue to the question 4 activities. It is our job, as educators, to have a process in place to determine who would most benefit from extension, which means determining the difference between a student's passion and mastery of a topic. When providing these extensions, it is important to consider students' voice and choice when developing ways for them to show this passion and mastery in a way that represents personalized learning. *Personalized learning* is an instructional approach designed to nurture learners to discover and broaden the ways they learn best by encouraging student voice, choice, and interest; this helps them master the highest standards possible in a relational environment and become independent learners committed to their learning (Weichel, McCann, & Williams, 2018). The key words in this definition are the *voice* and *choice* that students have in their learning.

Let's first gain some clarity around our purpose with this book, then we can move on to some discussion of how we organized it.

Clarity Around Purpose

There is an elephant in the room when it comes to dealing with question 4 students. Our goal in this introduction is to directly deal with that elephant and explain the rationale for our perspective on it. Let's first be clear about what an elephant in the room is. Most people are probably aware of the common expression, which means something that everyone knows about but that no one wants to address. As authors, we actually *do* want to talk about the problem, because in our consulting work with schools and teacher teams, this elephant always comes up when discussing how to answer question 4 in the PLC at Work process. The elephant in the room as it relates to question 4 students is both the positive and negative viewpoints that people have toward gifted education, issues around attaching gifted labels to students, and concerns related to challenging and supporting all students. We want to be clear: we believe that all students have gifts, and the point of this book is to allow for all students to shine and be challenged in the areas in their education where they are proficient or exceed learning expectations or targets. This book will give teacher teams practical ways to assess and then challenge all their students in a purposeful and efficient manner.

As authors, we believe that we cannot move forward in discussing our ideas on how to best support question 4 students without discussing this elephant in our room. When we visit with other educators about question 4, we hear questions like these.

- "Are we talking about gifted students?"
- "Are we adding more labels to our students?"
- "Isn't this supposed to be about supporting all kids, not just one group?"

We believe that everyone on a collaborative team has wrestled with these kinds of questions when thinking about answering PLC question 4 with students, yet often teams are not able to reach consensus or have honest discussions about their beliefs related to these questions. Our stance is that these questions are legitimate and deserve answers. These questions summarize question 4's elephant in the room and should be discussed first so that teachers are all on the same page on how to best approach their question 4 students.

Gifted Students

Our mindset on personalized learning within the structure of the PLC at Work process is one that believes strongly in students demonstrating mastery rather than receiving a label such as *gifted*. Gifted education is certainly a reality in our schools, and we created this book not to stop it but rather to support it. We ask educators to consider possibly taking some of the strengths of gifted education programs and applying them for all students, not just a select few who are identified depending on where they live and where they go to school. We fully recognize that due to societal pressures and community expectations, gifted education is unlikely to go away (although many school systems have moved away from it), but we do advocate setting up a system that is personalized for students and focuses on mastery. We believe that the current research (Lockhart, Meyer, & Crutchfield, 2022; Peters, Carter, & Plucker, 2020) and practices in gifted education can actually support why personalized learning is so essential for our students.

Professor and researcher Scott Peters is recognized nationally as an expert on the current research and practices in gifted education. Peters, during a podcast discussion with cognitive psychologist and author Scott Barry Kaufman (2019), maintains that there are two ways to improve gifted education in the United States. The first is a long-term solution that would fix the opportunity gap for students early in their education career. This solution is grounded in front-loading more gifted and talented opportunities for students at young ages, especially in low-income areas, as these students are often unidentified. In a PLC at Work school, where teams embrace the process of answering question 4 for *all* students, students in all grade levels (starting in early childhood and primary grades, and regardless of their income level) receive regular opportunities to extend their learning when it makes sense for them based on their current knowledge, skill levels, and readiness levels. The second way that Peters (Kaufman, 2019) proposes for gifted education to improve is to find a way to provide students who need more right now with extended learning. Simply stated, the concept is this: the student, having mastered *x*, now needs to learn *y*. This concept of providing right-now learning extension is the essence of personalized learning. We believe that addressing question 4 with your collaborative team can support both of Peters's (Kaufman, 2019) solutions that gifted education needs, and all students will benefit from doing so.

Most gifted education programs rely on test scores and national norms for students to qualify. Peters, along with colleagues Karen Rambo-Hernandez, Matthew

C. Makel, Michael S. Matthews, and Jonathan A. Plucker (2019) share that "the difference between gifted education and other areas of exceptional student education is that the procedures for deciding which students are served in gifted education vary widely across and within states" (p. 2). Essentially, this means that one student could be identified as gifted in one school system, but the same student might not be identified that way at a different school district just a few miles away. Peters and his colleagues (2019) contend that gifted programs should not rely on national norms and instead consider local norms, building by building. While we certainly agree that this identification process is far better for students when done locally as opposed to being based on national norms, we believe that educators should take this a step further—to the classroom and to the grade-level team. Why not base qualification for extended learning on what students demonstrate in each classroom? Why not base qualification for deeper learning on a specific unit or topic on what the student actually knows and doesn't know? What if teacher teams had common formative assessments for each unit that gave them insight into what the students already know, and they could then personalize their learning based on this insight? Again, this is the essence of the personalized learning approach that we advocate within the PLC at Work process. See table I.1 for a summary of the differences between typical gifted education programs and the question 4 practices that we propose.

TABLE I.1: Differences Between Gifted Education Programs and Question 4 Practices

Gifted Education Practice	Question 4 Practice
Criteria vary state by state, district by district.	Criteria are the same for all classrooms in each grade level.
Criteria are based on national norms.	Criteria are based on norms determined at the grade and classroom level.
Student is labeled as gifted for the long term.	Student is considered a question 4 student for the short term based on a common assessment.
Student is labeled as gifted in all subjects.	Student is considered a question 4 student skill by skill, subject by subject.
Student gets extended learning opportunities in fragmented time frames.	Student gets extended learning opportunities when necessary.

Labels

In education, we have a label—often accompanied by an acronym—for everything under the sun. One of the hardest parts about being a new staff member in a given school district is wrapping your head around all of the commonly used labels, phrases, and acronyms that your colleagues use with great ease. We are aware of school districts that actually provide new staff members with a listing of all of these different labels and acronyms so that new staff have more help in understanding this hidden language. Labels, in instances like these, can be both good and bad, depending on your experience as a staff member and on how educators in the school actually use the labels. We believe the same to be true with labels for students. Having said that, we do want to acknowledge that some view labeling students as a harmful practice and have a valid rationale for that view. Let's dig a little deeper into this elephant.

Some labels and acronyms that are commonly used in education (IEP [individualized education plan], 504, EL [English learner], and Title IX, for example) were established in order to provide students with equitable experiences, opportunities, and access. We believe that educators can agree that keeping equity in mind is not only a good but also a morally correct practice. We wish that labels didn't have to exist for students, but we are glad for them because they can help students receive the best chance possible to be successful and have equal access and rights to the best educational opportunities there are. But there is a downside to these labels, despite the well-intentioned purpose of them. The Individuals With Disabilities Education Act (IDEA) went into law in 1975 to ensure that "children with disabilities have opportunities to develop their talents, share their gifts, and contribute to their communities" (United States Department of Education, n.d.). IDEA was never meant to provide an avenue to generalize about certain students and put limits on their potential.

Our colleagues and friends Jeanne Spiller and Brian Butler (2020) wrote a wonderful blog post about the harm that labeling can cause. In short, Jeanne and Brian share that when students have labels, it causes teachers to lower their expectations for that student—even unconsciously. For example, a teacher might think, "Oh, that student has a hard time reading, I won't ask much of her." Or, when another student has a hard time learning mathematics facts, "I'll ask him to help me organize the classroom instead." What a teacher thinks about a student is likely going to become reality; high expectations get high results. Day by day and year after year, lowered expectations create a tremendous gap between those who can and those who can't. In fact, education professor and researcher John Hattie and his colleagues' (2017) metastudy of factors that impact student achievement shows that there are few things more important than teacher estimates of achievement. In fact, on the list of variables, only collective teacher efficacy and self-reported grades garnered a higher ranking (Hattie et al., 2017).

Remember the familiar phrase that the city of Las Vegas once used to attract visitors? "What happens in Vegas, stays in Vegas." It originated in a tourism department marketing meeting in 2003 (May, 2014), a snapshot of a time before virtually every citizen in the world is a potential journalist who can post pictures, blogs, podcasts, and social media posts on a moment's notice. When you post something on Facebook or Twitter, it is there for the entire world to see. Even if you personally delete it later, people may still be able to find it—whether you want that to happen or not. You may have seen one or more examples of this happening in aspects of your life.

The method of labeling we suggest is, to use social media terminology, a little like the app Snapchat, which allows users to share items that are visible for a short time and then disappear without being archived. We quickly determine question 4 students for a moment, providing them the right opportunity or extension, and then the label is gone. Unlike traditional labeling, with our question 4 approach, no long-term labels exist. Showing what they know and can do in one subject area allows students to work on an alternate or extended assignment for the duration of that unit. This approach is more about opportunities and less about labels.

All Students

When looking at gifted programming models, there are plenty of options to choose from. They include:

- Full-time services and schools for the gifted
- Supplementary programs outside the school day
- Pull-out or push-in programs
- Subject-area placement or acceleration
- Cluster grouping
- Personalized learning units in which students have voice and choice

All these models have advantages and disadvantages, depending on one's viewpoint, beliefs, and rationale. As advocates for all students, it is very clear to us as educators and authors which model resonates most. In short, we are believers in personalized learning. We would contend that the personalized learning approach that is best for all students is short-cycle cluster grouping (Hattie, 2008). These short-cycle cluster groups, based on what students know (via a preassessment), last for individual units of instruction, are flexible, and provide immediate support. This book will allow for the readers to develop short-cycle cluster groups in the midst of units to meet the needs of all learners in their classrooms.

The PLC process is based on teams of teachers collaborating and applying the four critical questions to *all* their students—not just some of them. Additionally, teacher teams typically spend the bulk of their time, understandably, on the first three PLC questions, and they often push question 4 to the side. We created this book to support teacher teams in simplifying extensions and giving concrete ways to support question 4 students. As authors, we contend that question 4 should always be applied, unit by unit, to all students—regardless of a student's label.

Perhaps most exciting is that we believe focusing on question 4 unit by unit will begin to change negative historical trends. Sadly, disproportionate rates in education along racial and ethnic lines in areas such as discipline rates, test scores, honors classes and gifted education programs, and many others have been well documented and researched (de Brey et al., 2019; Kaufman, 2019). In the area of gifted education, there has been considerable debate in the United States about traditional practices in determining which students qualify for gifted education programs with criticism that these programs tend to be geared toward students who are White, Asian American, or from high-income backgrounds (Dreilinger, 2020; Yoon & Gentry, 2009). Providing opportunities for some groups of students and not others can have tremendous cultural and economic implications if they remain unaddressed, and doing so is just wrong (Kaufman, 2019). When deserving students don't receive the formal opportunity to learn and grow in a personalized manner like their peers, we are not meeting the needs of all learners. Imagine the contributions of high-performing students from marginalized communities that we have lost because of the formal education systems that we have put into place.

As author Yvette Jackson (2021) describes, gifted education programs were developed to address students who are really going to make a contribution to the world based on test scores, and Title I programs focus on teaching students who are in deficit, also based on test scores. This system is flawed because we know students are more than just numbers. A negative effect of this thinking is that students, schools, and districts receive permanent labels, which highlights the type of education they receive. Students labeled as discipline issues or from poor families are funneled into traditional systems that can contribute to negative outcomes and are too often associated with students who are not White and not middle or upper-middle class (Kelly, 2019; Mineo, 2021).

The systems described in this book support the work of educators by avoiding permanent labels and not falling into the mind trap of excluding certain students who show talent because they haven't always shown talent in school (Weichel et al., 2018).

Just like personalized learning concepts, identifying students who already know it in each unit is enormously beneficial to them, especially for those who are members of marginalized communities; doing so is a key tool for reducing the achievement gap.

The reality, based on our experience and in working with educators around the country, is that students who frequently need question 4 support have been shortchanged for years. This happens because not many educators and teams have spent time thinking about them, their needs, and how they can best grow. In some cases, they have been unconsciously overlooked by well-meaning educators. In other cases, they have been intentionally ignored due to struggling students receiving higher priority from individual teachers, collaborative teams, or entire school systems. When it comes to instructional delivery, probably no cohort of students in our experience has received less consideration in the American school system. This group of students will still be proficient even if teachers don't make them a priority. While it may not be best practice, it's certainly understandable that teacher teams, schools, and school districts tend to take on a mindset that these students won't excel, but they will be fine; nobody will really notice. Teachers often ask students who are already proficient to serve as assistants, helping out with classroom tasks and even tutoring other students who are struggling. What if question 4 students don't *want* to just be helpers? Don't they deserve to be challenged in their own learning? What would you want for your own children if they were question 4 students in a specific unit of learning?

We argue that these students aren't in fact satisfied with being helpers; they do want and need to be challenged. Although school often comes easy to students who already know it, it is not uncommon for students who fit this description to feel comfortable playing the "game" of school and at the same time experience anxiety while striving for perfection. Proficient students who aren't challenged may fall into what psychologist and author Carol Dweck (2015) calls a fixed mindset. In school, a fixed mindset can manifest in high-achieving students when they are more concerned about looking smart and have less regard for learning. In contrast, students with a growth mindset are more concerned about learning and can deal with struggle, as opposed to focusing on grades. A large body of research shows that students with a growth mindset are more likely to perform better in school and beyond. Put simply, all students need to be challenged, pushed, and given opportunities to grow (Dweck, 2015).

Therefore, here are the central questions that we believe teams, schools, and districts should consider.

- What if there were a system in place in which collaborative teams made a collective commitment and team norms to regularly consider question 4 students?

- What if these teams had an easy-to-use toolbox from which, in every unit, they collaboratively chose a preassessment and matching strategy that would work just right for the question 4 students in their class?
- What if teams could set the bar schoolwide for how they address the needs of all learners?

We believe intentional work on behalf of question 4 students also benefits the entire classroom. When creating deliberate systems for extension, everyone wins. Students who know the material aren't just helpers; teams push and challenge them in their own learning. Teachers are able to provide more support to students who are struggling. Students who are right on track with their learning can receive new leadership opportunities. The teacher can enjoy an environment alive with the buzz of engagement and excitement where all students meet challenges at the level they need to ensure growth. Imagine an entire school system embracing this system. Schools exist to push, challenge, and grow *every* student. All students benefit from being uncomfortable—though not anxious—once in a while in their learning and being in a space where they don't know the answer (Warner, 2016). This rarely happens for question 4 students, and that's not without reason. Here are some of the rationales that we have seen for why this happens.

- Teachers lack sufficient time to prepare for question 4 students.
- The majority of the class and struggling students receive priority.
- Teachers aren't sure how to determine who already knows the content or skills they need to know and who doesn't.
- Teams don't have an intentional plan in place to support question 4 students.

About This Book

This book removes these barriers for your team and provides you with practical strategies to support question 4 students in ways that will not tax your team's time and resources. We do understand that the work in this book represents time, effort, and energy for teachers. With that understanding, we also believe that this time, effort, and energy are all well spent due to the impact they will have on all your students. We maintain that collaborative teams, working together, can build systems and protocols to make supporting proficient students easier and more efficient. Once this thinking and way of meeting the needs of all learners become routine, they will not cause such a time crunch. We also maintain that doing this work together as teams during regularly scheduled times is an efficient use of time.

We believe that teacher teams are committed to implementing engaging and thought-provoking activities for every student. High-performing teams, by their very nature, want to push, challenge, and prepare different students for each unit to expand who they consider question 4 students. We believe that every team should strive to ensure that every student should be a question 4 student on some unit of study during the year.

Our central premise in this book is not only to challenge question 4 students but to challenge you, the reader, as well. We challenge you and your team to just try one question 4 strategy this school year, or better yet, try all eight that we offer, one for every month of the school year. Teams might talk about trying to support question 4 students, but it often stops at talk. We created this book as a resource for teams to help them to get beyond talking about it and take action by trying a common preassessment and a strategy for extending the learning. This will create a great learning opportunity for your team. What worked and didn't work in the common preassessment? What can be done better next time? Teams can apply these same questions when implementing question 4 strategies. And here is the best part: even if you use these ideas and it doesn't work as well as you would have liked, you have lost nothing. Instead, you have gained a valuable team and student experience that ultimately will make your team better and more effective. Many teachers we work with share that they are nervous about the possibility that these ideas won't work well. When we ask what the question 4 students did last year during the same unit, the typical response is a rueful look along with an admission like, "Yeah, that's true. I have nothing to lose."

This book offers tools for all teachers to use to help make this happen. We aim to provide a resource broad enough to be useful to all teachers—no matter what grade level—while at the same time making it flexible and open enough to provide endless possibilities for learners. Each chapter contains one common preassessment and a corresponding question 4 strategy, with the idea that teams can proceed through the book and try out one of each at least once a month. We don't believe it is too much to ask a high-performing team to challenge itself to intentionally support all students in this way. While you can start and stop any time during the school year, we think that the best benefits will come to teams that use these resources throughout the school year—all eight strategies. Your team members can think of yourselves as interns of question 4 this year, as it certainly won't be a perfect process. The point is that you start and just try it.

Chapters 1–8 each feature one common preassessment and one question 4 strategy that you can pair for use with your class each month. For both the common preassessment and question 4 strategy, you will learn the specifics of the strategy, how you can use it in your classroom, and the step-by-step process your team could use to implement it. This process includes student handouts and planning guides to make this work as concise, explicit, and efficient as possible. These tools appear as figures to accompany the process descriptions of each strategy, and then reproducible versions of them appear at the close of each chapter for you to copy and use. To help you and your team envision how these common preassessments and strategies work in action, each chapter includes two concrete, detailed, real-life examples featuring teams from a variety of content areas and grade levels. These examples are intended to provide a glimpse at how other teams paired the common assessment with the question 4 strategy, which could spark inspiration for you and your team's planning. The intent isn't that you choose one of these and use it as described but that you treat them as resources to help shift your thinking as well as your actions.

The final chapter provides templates and tools that allow teams to look back on their eight-month trial and determine next steps, with reproducible versions available at the end of the chapter. Perhaps your team thinks the preassessment you used back in October would pair better with the question 4 strategy you just tried in April for the unit that starts in November. Whatever the preferred pairing and strategy might be, team members will do what great teachers do and reflect on what worked. Be honest about what didn't work, and plan for the upcoming year. Soon, addressing question 4 with regularity, common vocabulary, and passion will be the norm for your collaborative team. When this happens, all of your students benefit!

Closing and Reflection

Some years before he coauthored this book, Steve was finishing third grade at Winchester Elementary School in Northville, Michigan. He was identified as a "gifted" student for the following school year. While he doesn't remember the basis for this label, we can assume it was due to some sort of formula based on both his reading and mathematics scores on a nationally normed assessment, perhaps along with some teacher input. Looking back, it's clear to him that the reasons for being invited into the Plus Program—the name given to the gifted program at the time—had very little to do with giftedness and much more to do with his background. He was lucky to have a family that valued literacy and made it a regular part of its routine. For example, he had books read to him as a small child, received all sorts of help reading before he entered kindergarten, and he can still recall his mom quizzing him before every single Friday spelling test. Additionally, at a very young age and due to his father's passion for sports, he watched more football and baseball games on television than most kids his age—and had a newspaper delivered to the house daily, which gave him ample opportunities to read and pore over box scores daily. He began collecting baseball cards at the age of six (he still has the 1977 Topps baseball card set in his parents' basement) and spent more hours than he would like to admit staring at the statistics on the back of the cards.

So guess what happened to him? Compared to his peers, he could read, comprehend, spell, and compute faster and more accurately than most other students, and he was chosen to enter the Plus Program. He still remembers being excited for Friday spelling tests and for the various speed mathematics fluency tests, in which teachers kept track of how many correct answers a student could get in one minute. The combination of the skills he was good at with the competition was energizing to him as a student. Was he gifted? Did he have something that other students his age didn't have? He probably just had many more opportunities than others to practice reading and mathematics skills on things he liked (sports novels, baseball cards, the sports page in the newspaper, and much more). But there is more to this gifted story.

Once he entered this program in fourth grade, he was pulled out of his regular classroom to spend time with other gifted students and a specialized teacher. He didn't like the fact that he had to leave his classroom friends, and worse yet, he missed classroom experiences with his regular classroom teacher. Put simply, he wanted to be with his friends and didn't want to miss out on what the rest of the class was doing. Sometimes he participated in new learning activities when he was pulled out; other times, he did the same learning activities that he would have done in his regular classroom with the gifted program teacher and students. Other times, the program students took field trips to outside locations to learn about different science and history concepts. These were not subjects that Steve was particularly interested in at that time, and he certainly did not have a lot of background knowledge in these areas, as they were not in his wheelhouse of sports. Putting all these factors together, do you think a young Steve was enjoying his experience in the Plus Program? The answer is no. He still remembers getting onto a bus with other Plus Program students, traveling to another school in the district to join up with its gifted program students, and going through another boring activity, while missing out on what was happening back at his own school in his own classroom with his friends. After that day, he recalls going directly home and finally demanding that his mom remove him from the Plus Program because it just wasn't for him. Looking back, this was his first bad experience in his educational life. What lessons might we draw from this true story as it relates to personalized learning and providing the right support to a question 4 student?

- Steve would have benefited much more from opportunities to extend learning within his own classroom so that he could be with his classmates and his teacher or teacher team. Classroom community and the relationships student have with their teachers are powerful forces, and pulling students out of that community can sometimes hamper them and their outlook on learning. According to Hattie (2008), the classroom climate is critical for students in learning, and the student-teacher relationship is in the top fifteen of his identified high-impact variables. With the question 4 approach we are proposing that teachers and teacher teams engage in, you can do it all with the existing teachers in your classrooms.

- Instead of labeling a student as gifted based on fairly limited criteria that may or may not apply to the actual skills or concepts being taught (like Steve's science and social studies field trips), we propose that teacher teams create a system in which students are preassessed on the upcoming unit and if they qualify, they receive opportunities to extend learning. These systems can take into account students' voices and choices in the processes they use and the products they create.
- Lastly, we believe that every student is special and has gifts. By personalizing learning, we are not leaving students behind with labels—we are giving all students at one point or another the ability to display their gifts based on what they bring to the table at that time. For example, a student like Steve could have benefitted in his elementary experience from a personalization and extension strategy around sports or one of his other passions. Talk about a game-changing opportunity for all students!

We will close this chapter with an important quote from Hattie and his colleagues (2017) related to how we as educators have traditionally grouped our students:

> We have lost count of the number of times we have talked with well-meaning educators who hope that the solution to their students' achievement lies in grouping students by their perceived ability. Taking a grade level of students and giving one teacher the lowest performing students, another teacher average performing students, and yet another the highest performing students may be popular, but the evidence is clear that is it not the answer. . . . These sorts of rigid, long-term grouping are sometimes known as tracking and typically assume student learning needs and potential remain constant over time. This practice is not supported by research. But needs-based instruction, with flexible groups, should not be eliminated. (p. 226)

It is time for educators to support our question 4 students the right way, based on the evidence and research that is abundantly clear. Our goal with this book is to provide teacher teams with tools that make doable the practice of meeting the needs of all students. You just have to try it with your question 4 students.

CHAPTER 1

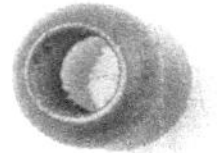 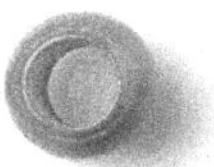 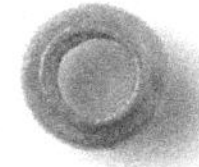   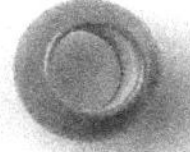 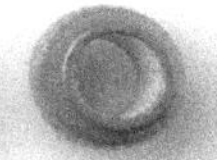

Showing What I Know With Inventories and Curriculum Compacting

What was middle school (grades 6–8) like for you? We focus on that time frame because many people think back to it as an awkward and self-conscious time of their lives. Coauthor Mark still remembers his first day of seventh grade, which was the first year of middle school where he grew up. He and some friends were walking together toward their old elementary school out of habit, only to realize that they were now big seventh graders. Mark would say that he made the mistake because he wanted the familiar, to see the students, teachers, and administrators who really knew him, and he was apprehensive about the unknowns that awaited him. Do you remember the walk or ride to school on your first day of middle school after summer vacation and that little feeling of nervousness and anxiety as you approached? Perhaps you weren't quite sure who your teacher would be, which friends would be in your class, where you would sit at lunchtime, or who you would hang out with between classes. For Mark, that nervous feeling washed away as soon as he saw his friends, the familiar parts of the school, and a friendly teacher greeting him at the door.

Relationships and how they feel are critical to any student's success in school, which is why it is so important for the adults who are responsible for the culture and climate of the classroom to intentionally learn about the learners in the room. All of us desire to be known and understood, and we believe that this is critical to support students.

When we see our teachers and school staff make an effort to learn about who we are and what we like, positive results occur. In our favorite book on this topic, *How to Teach Now* (Powell & Kusuma-Powell, 2011), the authors make the case that often, despite how important it is, we leave getting to know our students to chance or don't get to know them at all. In fact, getting to know students is as important a task as there is for educators. Building relationships creates a psychologically safe environment for every learner, determines each student's readiness for learning, identifies multiple access points to the curriculum to increase engagement and motivation, and develops and demonstrates greater emotional intelligence in the classroom (Powell & Kusuma-Powell, 2011). All these benefits are critical to providing resources for question 4 students not only for an individual unit but for the entire year. Inventories and curriculum compacting, the pair of strategies we have chosen for this chapter, are both ways to help teachers connect with their students on an individual level.

Preassessment: Inventories

One effective way to learn about students at the beginning of a school year is to use *inventories*—tools to find out more information about your students and what they know. We recognize that using inventories will look very different depending on whether you are a primary, intermediate, middle, or high school teacher. It also may look different based on your subject area and what kind of information you are seeking. Elementary teachers who are with the same group of twenty to thirty-five students all year compared to a secondary teacher with over one hundred students will have different demands. We would argue that regardless of the level, taking the time to ask the right questions and then doing something with what you learned on a regular basis will go a long way for you and your students. We are asking teams to create systems to get to know students in order to leave nothing to chance.

We think of inventories in two different ways. The first is learning about the students' likes and dislikes, strengths and weaknesses, and overall interests. Information gleaned from this type of tool will not only help you learn about the students you serve but also provide a glimpse into the future areas of study where they may already know content or skills during a later unit. Once you have conducted this type of inventory, we recommend developing a system of cataloging or even displaying information about the students. Of course, be careful about what you display for the entire classroom to see. Strengths, interests, learning styles, and learning preferences are generally acceptable for display, while things like grade reporting and other demographic information would not be. Our favorite resource for this type of inventory is the one created by writers and educators Barbara Bray and Kathleen McClaskey (2015), which seeks to determine students' strengths, challenges, preferences, and needs.

We have seen teachers do clever things like posting poster-sized information about students and their learning preferences so the list could be used as the year progressed when selecting students for teams. For example, one intermediate classroom we observed had a poster on the board with strengths drawn from a Gallup survey and individual student names clipped to the corresponding strength. With this poster, everyone in the classroom could see each other's top strength. Additionally, we have seen teacher teams use this information to work collaboratively to better support students based on their strengths, weaknesses, and learning interests. We have found that classrooms where students know about each other and use that information to help and support one another is a powerful learning tool. The ability to collaborate and work with others is one of the most sought-after career skills worldwide, and students must practice these skills in a safe environment; you can make your classroom a place to foster this practice. Students' abilities to work together, link multiple chains of logic, and tackle projects that are too cognitively demanding to complete alone serve a wide range of benefits in terms of both career and learning outcomes (Sparks, 2017).

The second type of inventory is designed to quickly determine what the student already knows about the unit you will be teaching. In a student handout, you and your collaborative team will list the key concepts, vocabulary, and skills students will need to know in this unit. Then, students will indicate with a plus, check, or X what they already know about the material. For example, if this is something that is new to them and they don't yet understand, students can just put an X. If it is something that they know a little about, they can put a check. If it is something that they know a great deal about, they can list a plus. For items with a plus, students would also indicate how they know about this topic.

For each of the eight chapters, asking students to complete this early common formative assessment before the unit is taught is just one piece to learning who the question 4 students are. With each unit, the teacher will want to follow up with the students and learn more about their knowledge and understanding of this unit. The document may look like the student does have a deep initial understanding; however, this needs to be clearly confirmed before they can be considered a question 4 student. We recommend the following steps for inventories.

1. Looking at the upcoming unit, brainstorm a list of the specific concepts, vocabulary, and ideas students will learn. List the items in figure 1.1 (page 18). See page 29 for the reproducible. If you have developed essential learning standards for the unit, please use that document as a resource to help guide the team.

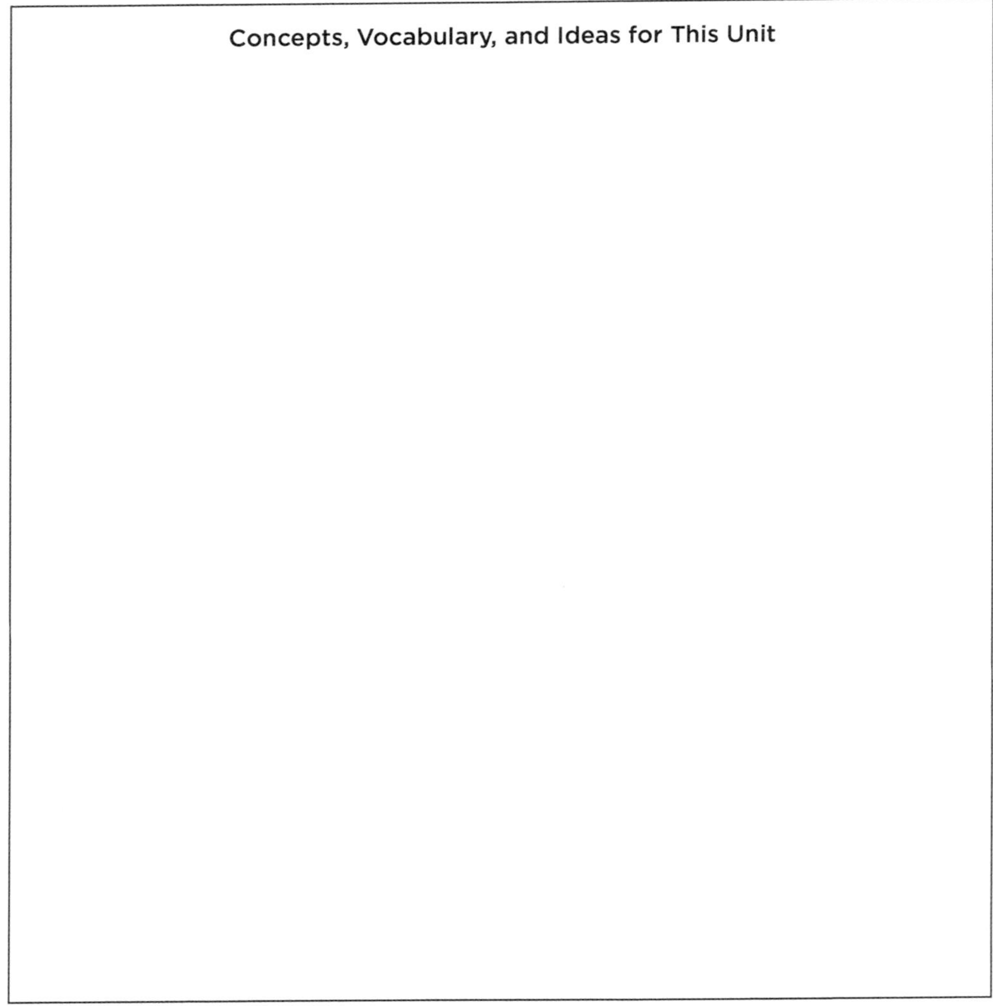

Figure 1.1: Concepts, vocabulary, and ideas that students will learn.

2. Determine which items from step 1 are the most important to consider for this unit.
3. List and number the most important items from step 1. Each numbered item will be an item for the left-hand column of the "I already know it" inventory student worksheet in figure 1.2.
4. Add the items to the "I already know it" inventory student worksheet.
5. Ask students to complete the "I already know it" inventory worksheet. See page 30 for a reproducible version.

Concepts, Vocabulary, and Ideas for This Unit	+ = I know a lot about this. ✓ = I know some things about this. X = This will be new learning for me.	If you recorded a +, share how you know about this topic.

Figure 1.2: "I already know it" inventory student worksheet.

6. Analyze the results of the inventories with your collaborative team. Determine which students could be considered question 4 students. As with any preassessment, a conversation with the students to confirm their level of understanding will be necessary.

Question 4 Strategy: Curriculum Compacting

We have found that differentiating curriculum and instruction is a challenging yet worthwhile task for all teachers. When differentiation doesn't take place for students who already know the material, they can quickly become bored, underperform, and even become disenchanted with their school experience. The challenge for teachers is to address the needs of all students—those who struggle *and* the question 4 students, who have many differences in areas such as interests, learning preferences, and academic ability.

One well-known and highly successful strategy that teachers can use to accomplish this is curriculum compacting. Curriculum compacting was first written about in 1979 when educational psychologists Joseph Renzulli and Linda H. Smith wrote *A Guidebook for Developing Individualized Education Programs (IEP) for Gifted and Talented Students*. This seminal work has been further researched and extended since its original publication. A detailed guide with examples of curriculum compacting we recommend is *Curriculum Compacting: A Guide to Differentiating Curriculum and Instruction Through Enrichment and Acceleration* (Reis, Renzulli, & Burns, 2016).

While there are many nuances and details to this model, *curriculum compacting* is basically when teachers look at the standards and indicators that they will teach in a certain time frame, and then they compact this learning into shorter segments based on the students' individual needs. For example, say a teacher is beginning to teach a unit on the Civil War to a group of eighth-grade students and has determined the key essential standards and outcomes. After a preassessment to see which students already know the material, the teacher then works with the students who demonstrate knowledge in this area. Based on what the preassessment shows, the teacher and each question 4 student complete a curriculum compacting contract. The contract shows what standards the class will cover, how the student has demonstrated knowledge of this area, and the alternative extension activity the student will do in place of the traditional instruction. The student then receives some freedom and opportunities to engage in different experiences during the class.

With compacting, the main idea is that time is now freed up for students to go deeper and learn specifics about the subject area at the same time their peers might be more involved in whole-class and small-group instruction. Students who have a curriculum compacted for them are challenged with self-directed learning activities, instructional materials that focus on specific skills, or projects that are higher order or address project-based learning.

In traditional curriculum compacting, teachers clearly indicate the standards and indicators that they will teach in a given subject area. The next step is to determine the students who have already mastered the material and have the potential to learn the material at a deeper level. We are not necessarily talking about a faster pace; this model does not mean moving to another unit or grade level. Third, teachers follow up with the student with some sort of measurement to determine what areas the student is already proficient in and in what areas the student may need more teaching or reinforcement. If a student is well versed on three of the four indicators the upcoming unit addresses, the student may want or even be required to join the class for instruction on that fourth indicator or learn in a different way to reach proficiency.

In competency-based learning models, a key area of focus is learning at one's own pace and moving through progressions. While we support this structure, we also see that this type of work requires entire schools and school systems to be aligned. We have seen well-intentioned teachers allow students to quickly move through the mathematics curriculum, for example, from one grade level to the next, only to determine later that students moved so fast they may not have retained much of the information they were supposed to learn—or that no well-planned course sequence was present at higher grade levels to support their fast ascent. We believe that if educators wait for competency-based models to be adopted in their district to address question 4 students, students will miss out for many years. Curriculum compacting is designed for individual teachers and their collaborative teams to challenge question 4 students regardless of whether any competency-based systems are developed in their district or not.

With the extended time they get as a result of compacting, students receive opportunities for self-directed activities. Examples of exciting learning experiences could include:

> small group, special topic seminars that might be directed by students or community resource persons, community based apprenticeships or opportunities to work with a mentor, peer tutoring situations, involvement in community service activities, and opportunities to rotate through series of self-selected mini-courses. (Reis & Renzulli, n.d.)

In our experience, we have enjoyed sharing one particular resource with teachers who ask for a list of choices they can provide students for what a final product might be. Westside Personalized iCreate (https://bit.ly/3G1aTKJ; Easton, n.d.) is a wonderful tool that shows many strategies, which include how to develop videos, collages, paintings, storytelling with visuals, infographics, podcasts, online discussions, videos, presentations, and portfolios. The Westside resource grew from the work of Andrew Easton (n.d.), who served as personalized learning coordinator at Westside Community Schools in Omaha, Nebraska. We like this resource because it is not a traditional list. When we taught, students created PowerPoints or posters, and that was about as far as we took any kind of deeper learning. As technology has developed further, students have an abundance of ways to demonstrate their learning that are unique, creative, and fun for the learner. Technology allows students to do anything that the experts are doing. And, with these tools, the audience doesn't just have to be the teacher or the class; it can be anyone in the world. Authentic audiences give feedback and guidance on how to grow even more. Each type of activity Easton (n.d.) offers links to a site where the student can receive directions on how to make this happen. You want to make a podcast? Here are three sites that help you make and share a podcast for free. Want to make a blog? Here are the directions. Sharing this site with students will help them see some final product examples that can support their work, and teachers link it to their strengths, interests, and likes.

Teachers can simplify the workflow between themselves and their students who are having their work compacted in what Reis and Renzulli (n.d.) call the *compactor*. This is simply the document that become the contract between the student and the teacher about which standards they will compact and then, in turn, take to a deeper level. The Broward County Public Schools' Gifted Resources for Teachers website (https://bit.ly/3JI5haw) offers a variety of tools and resources for teaches looking to use curriculum compacting to personalize and enrich learning for gifted students. The compactor takes the form of a graphic organizer in which column 1 is reserved for the key areas being covered, column 2 is for how the student knows this material, and column 3 is for how the teacher can accelerate or enrich this information. The compactor really becomes a contract between the student and the teacher. The contract indicates the following.

- You know this.
- Here is how we will know you know this.
- You will get more out of the learning experience by doing this.

We used these ideas and background of the compactor to develop our own contract, which we call the "I already know it" contract. In this document, teachers specify the standards and indicators they are addressing, how students have shown they already know it, how they will show what they have learned, and, last, how they will know what their grade will be. Students, particularly gifted students, want to know how the extension will impact their grade. When we were students, we used to worry about our grades, so we certainly understand why this would be a concern for our students. A student might ask, "Am I going to be doing a bunch of extra work and maybe get a worse grade than if I just took the traditional test?" That is the beauty of the contract. When students fully understand and receive assurance from their teacher on the front end that they will be completing a different assignment and that their grade will be based on submitting a quality product, this grade anxiety can be significantly reduced. This continues to send the student an important message: it's not about the grade; it's about the learning! The student can then focus on the learning and the final product and not wonder, "What grade will I get?" The grade will be the highest mark available based on your assessment system as long as they do what was agreed on in the contract. Students will truly get the sense that the teacher wants them to learn and show what they can do. We believe that using the following steps for curriculum compacting sends a very powerful message to the student in this situation.

1. Teachers complete the standards and indicators column of the "I already know it" contract, one item per row. This will become the standard form for this unit. Students will have their own individual "I already know it" contract for this unit with the same items in column 1, allowing for columns 2–4 to differ based on student interests and strengths. (See figure 1.3 on page 24 and page 31 for the reproducible version.)
2. After analyzing the inventory list and identifying students who might benefit from extension, a one-on-one meeting with each student in this category takes place. The student and teacher will complete the How I Know It column. Students share their background and knowledge in each of the indicator and standard areas. This conversation will inform the teachers about which students to include in curriculum compacting and for which areas.
3. Students receive the assignment to complete column 3, How Can I Show Extended Learning? Teachers share the iCreate website (Easton, n.d.) to help students generate ideas and thoughts about how they might want to extend their learning. Once completed, students review their work and ideas with the teacher, who offers suggestions and ideas for editing. If students are stuck or not able to generate ideas, the teacher asks probing questions to support students in developing an overall plan.

Unit: ____________ Student: ____________ Teacher: ____________

Standards and Indicators	How I Showed I Know It	How Can I Show Extended Learning?	How Will I Know My Grade?

Figure 1.3: "I already know it" contract.

4. Students receive the assignment to complete column 4, How Will I Know My Grade? Students are to reflect on how they would like the teacher to consider their grade based on the products they have determined. Once completed, students review their work and ideas with the teacher, who offers suggestions and ideas for editing.
5. Collaborative team members determine times during class lessons when students are allowed to work on extension activities. What areas are critical for question 4 students to be fully included in, and where can they focus their efforts in a different way, per the contract?
6. Allow students flexible time to work on the contract.
7. During the unit, teachers regularly check on the students' progress to ensure that they are addressing all questions and concerns. They regularly provide feedback and challenge students to produce thoughtful, quality work.
8. At the conclusion of the unit, teachers review the work completed and, with each student, determine if the contact was met and what the final grade should be based on the work.

Example 1: Sixth-Grade Science

A sixth-grade elementary collaborative team is beginning work on an upcoming unit in science where all students will be introduced to the periodic table of elements as a precursor to tackling standards on matter and its interactions. Each year during these lessons, they have lectures and readings, which are interspersed with a series of class labs in which students construct experiments and record and interpret the data they gather. The class-conducted experiments are typically fun and engaging for students. However, the collaborative team has noticed in the past that some students were already familiar with the elements and basically took over the small groups, doing the class experiments on their own, while other students just watched. These students became mini-teachers in the labs, and the teachers thought that challenging the students who already know the material in a different way would give different leadership opportunities to the students who don't typically lead.

To start the unit, the team gives each of the students a short inventory, which consists of key elements they will be studying and asks the students what they know about the elements they had listed. To their astonishment, they have three to four students in each class who are familiar with the elements and show this in their inventory.

After the teachers have a chance to review the inventories, they meet individually with each student to find out a little more. They ask questions such as, "How do you know so much about this topic already?" They also ask specific questions tied to the key standards and indicators they are teaching in the unit to gain a good understanding of what the students already know.

At the end of these conversations, the teachers share the "I already know it" contract with students from each class when they have determined that the students understand the material, and it becomes evident that extension would be beneficial. By completing the guide, the teacher and student both gain a clear understanding of which standards they will cover in the unit, how the student will demonstrate understanding, and how the teacher will provide a deeper understanding. The teacher shares some ideas and options for what the extension activity would be. After looking at and talking about various choices, the students decide they want to create their own experiments that they could then share with the class. These choices could be individual, or students could make them in small or even large groups. The elementary and secondary examples we provide in this book are samples of the type of extension activities we promote.

Also, because this group of students is very concerned about grades for this extension activity, the teacher shares some specifics to make sure there are no surprises. First, the students take the end-of-unit exam to see in what parts of the unit they would need a bit more teacher support. For areas where the students get the majority correct, they can pass the class assignments. For the areas they needed extra study, they can either take part in the full class discussions on that part of the topic or watch a prerecorded video the teachers had made from past years with a short quiz to demonstrate proficiency.

Once the unit test, video, and quizzes are completed, the students use the time in which the rest of the class does guided labs and experiments to complete a group assignment where they choose an element. The teacher then proactively shares a blank rubric with the students, and they collaboratively talk about what a good project would look like. They discuss how some basic information about each element, such as its number, symbol, cost, and everyday use, is important. The students and teacher agree that the majority of the grade would be determined with the work they complete in the experiment to demonstrate the use and power of their element, and what happens when other elements are combined with theirs. Of course, they have to write up any experiment on paper, and the teacher has to approve it before they actually conduct it to ensure safety. Students develop research projects that they eventually share with others, which could include the class, school, or even larger community, depending on the project that they complete.

Example 2: High School Government

A junior- and senior-level government team is meeting in August prior to their students reporting to school to look over their year-at-a-glance documents and begin putting together learning plans for their accompanying units. For this team, the learning plans they create for each unit consist of a desk-sized calendar where they note what will happen on each day of the unit, such as common formative assessments, summative assessments, reteaching, hook activities, anticipatory sets, simulations, and reviews. While the team didn't follow every day at the same pace, they generally stuck together on their activities.

Team members note that in previous years, there was a tremendous divide in student abilities and prior knowledge on topics related to government. They might go from one student who doesn't think about government at all or talk about it at home to others who have regular conversations about it and even intend to major in this topic in the near future in college. They talk about how to set the stage for this wide range of proficiency with a plan that will challenge all learners in this year's work. The idea they settle on is to use inventories at the start of each unit, and then use curriculum compacting to allow for personalization for students who already know the material.

On the first day of class, all teachers on the team give their students an inventory of the main topics they will study. Students then check the columns to describe what they know about the topic; if they state that they know a lot about it, they include information about how they know a lot about it. Once they have collected the inventories, the teachers sort the students to identify who is a potential question 4 student. With this list, the teachers follow up with each student and ask further probing questions to understand how well they know these areas. After one-on-one conversations, the teachers can see which students need an "I already know it" contract.

For these students, the teachers form a contract. First, the teachers list the key standards that students will learn in the left-hand column. On the right, the students and teachers complete the information that explains how the students have already demonstrated proficiency on this material. Then, the students receive the assignment to determine the ways they can take these standards to a deeper level.

After seeing options and ideas, the various question 4 students develop individual plans. One student asks for class time to view state and national legislative bodies in action through live webcams and write a report on his findings. Another student asks to do a report on legislative issues that were on track to be debated in the state's legislative session. And another student asks to set up a class Twitter account where she can follow the accounts of key politicians and report to the class when posts are connected to topics they are studying in class.

Chapter Reflection

In chapter 9 (page 127), you will review what you have learned and tried from each chapter to make future planning decisions to determine which strategies will work best for your team. To assist in this, consider the following questions after trying this strategy.

Preassessment Reflection Questions: Inventories

1. Did this strategy help your team identify question 4 students?
2. Did this strategy take a reasonable amount of teacher time to implement?
3. Did this strategy take a reasonable amount of classroom time to implement?
4. Can you see your team using this strategy for future units to determine which students already know the material?

Question 4 Strategy Reflection Questions: Curriculum Compacting

1. Were students able to succeed as a result of this strategy?
2. Was this strategy easy for teachers to use?
3. Was this challenging for students?
4. Was this engaging for students?
5. Can you see your team using this strategy for future units to challenge students who already know the material?

Concepts, Vocabulary, and Ideas That Students Will Learn

Concepts, Vocabulary, and Ideas for This Unit

"I Already Know It" Inventory Student Worksheet

Concepts, Vocabulary, and Ideas for This Unit	+ = I know a lot about this. ✓ = I know some things about this. X = This will be new learning for me.	If you recorded a +, share how you know about this topic.

"I Already Know It" Contract

Unit: ________________ Student: ________________ Teacher: ________________

Standards and Indicators	How I Showed I Know It	How Can I Show Extended Learning?	How Will I Know My Grade?

CHAPTER 2

Showing What I Know With Multiple-Choice Quizzes and Choice Boards

In this chapter, since we're still early in the book, we wanted to start the work for you and your teams with a preassessment and corresponding question 4 activity that would be familiar and comfortable. Anyone who has been involved with formal schooling in one manner or another is certainly familiar with multiple-choice quizzes. We remember taking hundreds, if not thousands, of these types of tests over our school careers. Generally speaking, we were always prepared to take our quizzes in class, unless they were pop quizzes—students' least favorite type of quiz. Pop quizzes felt brutal to us and it always seemed as though the teacher wanted to get back at the students for one reason or another. In fact, on a few occasions, we can say with certainty that this was why the teacher administered it. How do we know this? The teacher told the class straight out that the pop quiz was punishment.

With the bad reputation of pop quizzes in mind, we want to make the argument that under the right circumstances, they can be enormously useful and beneficial. Of course students who take pride in their grades and performance in school aren't going to feel comfortable right away with taking a test they aren't prepared to do well on. Offering a small sample-size multiple-choice quiz to students before actually teaching the content might seem like punishment to some. The difference with this type of assessment is that while most students won't perform well, we wouldn't expect them to. Quickly learning what students know and are able to do before the unit begins is a simple and easy way for collaborative teams to determine what students already know before teaching a unit. The key is that teachers who provide this sort of a quiz before teaching the unit have a responsibility to be honest with the students about the purpose of the assessment. Make it clear to the students that there may be questions that they don't know the answer to, that this will not have an impact on their grade, and that you are using the information from the quiz to provide the best learning experience possible for the unit. Don't ever underestimate the importance of honest and open messaging between you and your students.

For busy teachers who are already working full schedules, the best part about the preassessment and strategy in this chapter is that they are doable with materials and resources that might already exist. If you are on teams similar to those we have been part of, you already have multiple-choice assessments in place. If that is the case, you could use this chapter as a resource to fine-tune your current assessment and determine which items would be best to use or modify for a preassessment. For teams without pre-existing multiple-choice assessments, this preassessment, paired with choice boards, will be a wonderful tool to begin your work. We discuss both in this chapter.

Preassessment: Multiple-Choice Quizzes

For any assessment, and particularly the preassessment you will be using for this unit, we recommend determining the overall purpose of the assessment and the appropriate "levels of thinking" that you will be using for your final item development. In our experiences, cross referencing your team's items with Benjamin S. Bloom's (1954) *Taxonomy of Educational Objectives* (see Anderson & Krathwohl, 2001, & Armstrong, 2010) with Norman L. Webb's (2002, 2009) Depth of Knowledge (DOK) is recommended as a way to evaluate and ensure you have a match between your standards, instructional methods, and assessments. As a quick reference guide for your team, we share an overview of these seminal works in figure 2.1, figure 2.2, and figure 2.3.

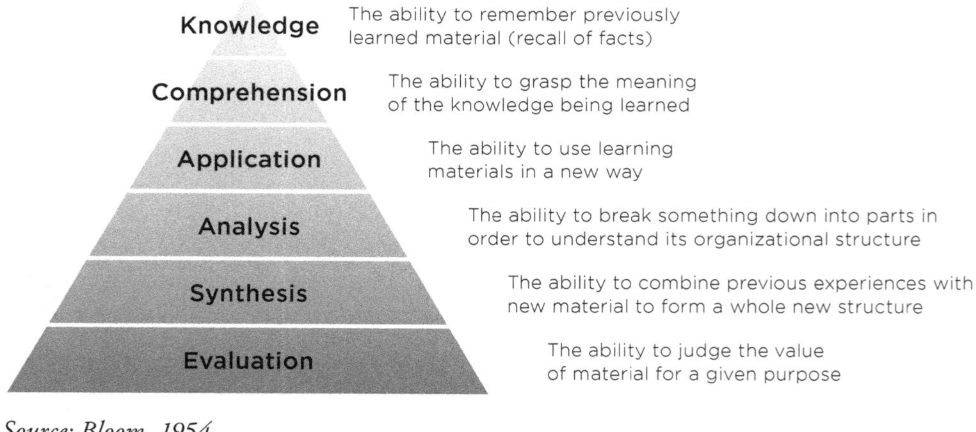

Source: Bloom, 1954.

Figure 2.1: Bloom's original taxonomy.

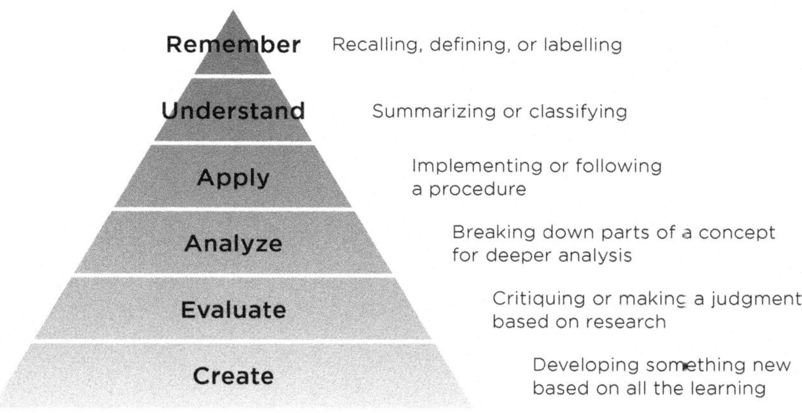

Source: Anderson & Krathwohl, 2001.

Figure 2.2: Bloom's updated taxonomy.

1. **Recall:** Requires recall of fact, information, or procedure	2. **Skill or concept:** Requires use of information of conceptual knowledge, two or more steps, and so on	3. **Strategic thinking:** Requires reasoning, developing a plan or a sequence of steps, some complexity, and more than one possible answer	4. **Extended thinking:** Requires an investigation and time to think and process multiple conditions of the problem

Source: Webb, 2002.

Figure 2.3: Webb's Depth of Knowledge.

If your final assessment and teaching methods ask for recall, then the preassessment multiple-choice quiz should reflect that. If your final assessment seeks higher-order thinking, your assessment should also match that. The multiple-choice preassessment we are suggesting is not intended to be an all-encompassing test to determine everything that a student knows about a specific subject area. Instead, it should give you a quick glimpse to help you determine which students might already know this material. Some of you may be looking at this suggestion and wondering how to make a short multiple-choice assessment if your course relies heavily on higher levels of thinking. Our biggest word of advice when creating the preassessment is to make it simple; don't overthink it. What will tell you quickly what students in the room may already know about the material? When you see how students perform, you can then circle back around and ask deeper, more thought-provoking questions.

For teams reading this and thinking this will be a difficult challenge because the assessments for the unit require higher-order thinking, there are resources and techniques to make multiple-choice tests match these challenges. Instructional designer Mike Dickinson (2011) writes about taking a concept and determining ways of asking multiple-choice questions based on each of the levels of Bloom's taxonomy. Our favorite resource for developing multiple-choice questions that require higher-order thinking comes from the Blended Learning Resources (n.d.) website. This site offers four practical and understandable strategies, which include using two-tier multiple-choice questions, real-world scenarios and case studies, analysis of visuals, and our favorite, multilogical thinking questions. We are confident that teams seeking to write these types of questions will view this as a powerful tool for writing higher-order questions.

Teams should consider best-practice suggestions for test construction, such as using only one correct option, giving clear instructions, clearly defining the problem and including the main idea in the question, keeping the item short and uncomplicated, and considering the reading level of the student (Painter, 2004). With these ideas in mind, this book is not intended to address specific models for multiple-choice test construction. For this type of guidance, there are many great books and resources that best demonstrate student learning through assessments; our favorites include *Classroom Assessment and Grading That Work* (Marzano, 2006) and *School Improvement for All: A How to Guide for Doing the Right Work* (Kramer & Schul, 2017). That said, we recommend the following steps for multiple-choice preassessments.

1. Identify the unit in which you will use this strategy.
2. Complete the preassessment planning chart by level of thinking in figure 2.4. See page 45 for a reproducible version.

   Think of column 1 as the various parts to a unit. For a unit covering colonialism and the American Revolution, this might be broken up by thinking about the main topics for this unit. For column 2, consider how many questions you will use to cover this unit on the summative assessment for each area. Your preassessment needs to consist of significantly fewer questions than this. From our experience, teachers can achieve a quick glimpse with a few questions per area. In the next two columns, reflecting on the thinking level required for students by referencing the work of Bloom and Webb will provide teams with a game plan for the types of questions necessary, which appear in the last two columns. A completed first row might look like figure 2.5 for an eighth-grade American history teacher.

Sections in Your Final Assessments	Multiple-Choice Questions for Each Section	Range of Bloom's Taxonomy	Range of DOK Levels	Types of Preassessment Questions	Ideal Number of Preassessment Items

Figure 2.4: Multiple-choice planning chart by level of thinking.

Sections in Your Final Assessments	Multiple-Choice Questions for Each Section	Range of Bloom's Taxonomy	Range of DOK Levels	Types of Preassessment Questions	Ideal Number of Preassessment Items
Pre-colonial times	Eight questions	Knowledge level	Level 1 and 2	Recall types of questions	Two questions

Figure 2.5: Multiple-choice planning chart by level of thinking example.

3. Based on the findings from the completed chart, begin constructing your multiple-choice preassessment. If the team already has a multiple-choice test that it typically uses at the end of the unit, members may determine which items they could use to best determine what students know.
4. Administer the preassessment to the entire class.
5. Score the preassessment, looking for students who already have a clear understanding of the subject matter. Place question 4 students' preassessments in one stack to take to an upcoming collaborative team meeting.
6. Share question 4 students with the collaborative team, and discuss if any further follow-up will be necessary with those students. If you are unsure about any students, a simple three- to five-minute conversation with each one may give you further insight into who is ready to participate in the question 4 strategy. Then you can begin to develop the question 4 choice board strategy for the unit.

Question 4 Strategy: Choice Boards

Many, if not all, of the strategies and ideas we share in this book are good for all learners. We would argue that personalized learning and offering voice and choice to students are strategies that engage and motivate students in classrooms at all levels and subject areas. In personalized learning classrooms, we have found that one of the simplest entry points is the use of choice boards. As many of these strategies are inspired by personalized learning practices, choice boards are a perfect fit. The choice board is advisable because it is a simple strategy that provides many options for teacher teams, and in turn, for students. It also allows teachers to be creative, and it can provide students with different learning modality options.

When looking to provide direction on creating choice boards, we have looked to the work of a few authors who have expertise in the area of blended learning and empowering students, all elements of a quality personalized learning classroom. Educator and speaker Catlin Tucker (2016) provides guidance for developing both online and offline choice boards. Online choice boards provide links to different online tools that are necessary to complete the learning activity. Offline choice boards allow for students to do an activity that doesn't require specific technology; they may require merely an old-school paper and pencil. Tucker (2016) writes in a blog post that when working with teachers on developing strategies to provide differentiation, student choice, and assessment, choice boards weave these elements into one.

Educator A. J. Juliani (2020) is another author who advocates implementing choice boards. He contends that choice boards are an effective way to increase student engagement due to the choice that they provide students. Increasing student engagement around learning standards and skill development is why we believe so strongly in personalized learning and why the use of choice boards can be effective.

So, what exactly is a choice board? A *choice board* is simply a graphic organizer featuring different learning activities that are based on a skill or standard as determined by the teacher team. Choice boards are typically organized in a tic-tac-toe format with nine different options for the student. While this format is popular, teacher team members certainly have the freedom to choose the format of their choice board, as they may want to provide more or fewer options. Choice boards that are not in the tic-tac-toe format are often called bingo choice boards. The key to making a useful and learning-focused choice board is to connect the activities that the students are to complete to the key standards or main skills that the teacher teams expect the students to learn.

There are many ways that teachers can use choice boards. If your team chooses to set up the choice board in a tic-tac-toe format, we have seen these sort of options.

- Students must choose three learning activities in a row: down, across, or diagonal, their choice.
- Students get a free space in the middle and have to choose two options in order to get three squares in a row.
- Students are required to complete specific squares (as determined by the teacher team) but get choice on the remaining squares.
- Students are required to complete three in a row, but the middle square is a *you decide* option and students can choose any square on the board to count as the middle square.

If your team uses a bingo choice board, we have seen these kinds of options.

- Students are required to complete a set amount of squares but get to choose which ones they prefer.
- Students are required to complete a certain number of squares in a row but get to choose the specific squares and direction they would like to go.
- Students are required to complete all of the squares except for one or two squares of their choice.
- The teacher team determines different point values for each activity in each square and students are required to do squares that equal a certain number of points.

Another novel approach to choice boards is to provide multiple learning activities that are organized based on levels of complexity or on a learning menu. In the level concept, teachers develop a small continuum of activities ordered by rigor or complexity. Students can choose one activity from each level (level 1, level 2, level 3, and so on) as they progress through the choice board. Similarly, in the menu process, teachers develop activities for each part of the menu and students have choice within each part of the menu in order to move on to the next menu item. Here are the steps we recommend for choice boards.

1. Through the use of the multiple-choice preassessment, determine who the question 4 students are on the grade-level team.
2. Determine your choice board approach: (1) tic-tac-toe, (2) bingo, (3) level, or (4) menu.
3. With your collaborative team, use the choice board brainstorm document and brainstorm a list of activities related to the standards being learned that could be considered for a choice board (see figure 2.6 and page 46 for the reproducible version). We believe team members should also discuss how they will assess these activities so that the team is on the same page.

Standard	Choice Board Activity	How Assessed?

Figure 2.6: Choice board brainstorm document.

4. Organize the activities based on the choice board approach you choose.
5. Based on the choice board approach you choose, determine your expectations for student completion.
6. Allow students to complete the choice board and assess or provide student feedback as needed.
7. After the choice board experience, ask students what activities they enjoyed the most, what had the most impact on their learning, and which ones they did not enjoy or value. The same process of questions should happen with the teacher team in order to collect feedback in preparation for using these boards next time.

Example 1: First Grade

A first-grade team of three teachers is planning their next unit. The purpose of the unit is for the students to learn about the main idea and supporting details in a text. The teachers collaborate before the unit begins and create a simple multiple-choice quiz from the student text. The quiz allows them to preassess how ready students are to determine the main idea from each paragraph and the supporting details for each main idea. As part of the learning process for the preassessment to assist them when taking the quiz, the teachers ask students to identify any main ideas by underlining and instruct them to put a smiley face in the text with any supporting details. After administering the short multiple-choice quiz, the teacher team is able to determine from the results what students understand and whether they can demonstrate proficiency on the concept of the main idea and supporting details.

The team not only identifies question 4 students, they also identify students who they deem on grade level and approaching grade level based on the agreed-on proficiency scale for the preassessment. Once the students are all identified, each group receives its own choice board, which the team differentiates for each group.

For example, the approaching-grade-level group's choice board has simplified activities like creating a main idea and supporting detail web and other graphic organizer options via technology possibilities like Google Drawing. Some of the choice board graphic organizers for this group include the main idea, and the student only has to determine the supporting details—a small step of scaffolding for the students who are approaching grade-level expectations.

The on-grade-level choice boards feature some of the same options as the approaching-grade-level group, except with no scaffolding supports. Additionally, their choice boards include different technology options and applications. For instance, students receive choice board options to record themselves explaining the main idea and supporting details and another option to make a video about the main idea and details.

Lastly, the question 4 students receive a few of the approaching-grade-level options with modifications that would give them more challenges. For instance, one of the options is for the students to listen to passages at the second- and third-grade reading levels using TumbleBooks (www.tumblebooklibrary.com) and then determining the main idea and supporting details from this audio experience.

This first-grade team example demonstrates how a team can take the concept of the multiple-choice quiz and choice boards, create a quality preassessment, and pair it with a challenging learning experience for all students, including the question 4 students in the class. We, as authors, are excited to hear how other teacher teams use this and other strategies as a starting point and get creative to better support their students.

Example 2: Seventh-Grade Science

A seventh-grade science team is preparing for its next unit on measurement. The essential standard driving this unit is that students should be able to measure with accuracy and precision. As the team discusses how to support students in the unit, members decide to give all students a ten-question multiple-choice quiz to determine where the students are with their measurement skills. They pull the quiz questions from a standardized assessment and then review them to ensure that the questions will help them know if students are able to properly measure or not.

After giving the quiz, the team gathers and divides the students into three groups.

- **Group 1:** Students who did poorly on the quiz and need further support
- **Group 2:** Students who made common errors
- **Group 3:** Students who demonstrated mastery in the quiz (question 4 students)

The team develops plans for all three teachers to execute in their individual classrooms. They are strategic in developing activities and instruction for groups 1 and 2 that will provide more individual teacher support. For group 3 students, the focus is to give them choices that will tap into their interests and that they can do independently with built-in teacher checkpoints every two to three days. In order to ensure that the students will be more independent in group 3, the teachers also create several short videos of common places where students might get stuck (based on what they experienced the previous year when they did this unit) so that students could review the videos first before needing to talk with the teacher. Last year, one of the teachers on the team also created a Google Doc with links for students who had challenges. This Google Doc, coupled with the videos that the teacher creates, gives the group 3 students plenty of independence and allows them to also work on their scale drawings and models at home if they choose to.

The strategy that the team uses for group 3 is a tic-tac-toe choice board. Students in group 3 are tasked with doing two scale activities while using the free space in the middle. Any direction the students choose will require them to complete one scale drawing and one scale model. The individual teachers set aside twenty minutes of class time every three days to check in with the students in group 3. Figure 2.7 is an example of one team's choice board (and yes, this school is in suburban Chicago!).

Build a scale model of Wrigley Field.	Using the scale model of a home, with the existing square footage, please add an additional bathroom on the second floor and a half bathroom on the main floor.	Create a scale model of our school. One new classroom must be added to the school to make room for a higher enrollment of students.
A model home has been built in a new neighborhood. The scale model does not have a garage on the home. Determine where the garage will go and create a scale drawing of it attached.	Free space	Build a scale model of the Willis Tower (the building formerly known as the Sears Tower).
Build a scale model of the United Center.	Build a scale model of Soldier Field.	The local Portillo's restaurant needs to be modified for less in-person dining and more drive-through space. Create a scale drawing that will add more drive-through space and less dining space with the existing square footage

Figure 2.7: Example of a tic-tac-toe choice board for a seventh-grade science class.

Chapter Reflection

In chapter 9 (page 127), you will review what you have learned and tried from each chapter to make future planning decisions and determine which strategies will work best for your team. To assist in this, consider the following questions.

Preassessment Reflection Questions: Multiple-Choice Quizzes

1. Did this strategy help your team identify question 4 students?
2. Did this strategy take a reasonable amount of teacher time to implement?
3. Did this strategy take a reasonable amount of classroom time to implement?
4. Can you see your team using this strategy for future units to determine which students already know the material?

Question 4 Strategy Reflection Questions: Choice Boards

1. Were students able to succeed as a result of this strategy?
2. Was this strategy easy for teachers to use?
3. Was this challenging for students?
4. Was this engaging for students?
5. Can you see your team using this strategy for future units to challenge students who already know the material?

Multiple-Choice Planning Chart by Level of Thinking

Sections in Your Final Assessments	Multiple-Choice Questions for Each Section	Range of Bloom's Taxonomy	Range of DOK Levels	Types of Preassessment Questions	Ideal Number of Preassessment Items

Choice Board Brainstorm Document

Standard	Choice Board Activity	How Assessed?

CHAPTER 3

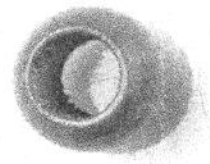 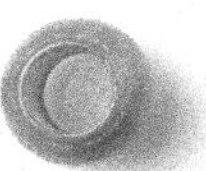 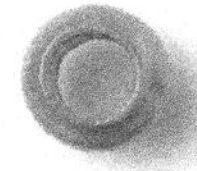  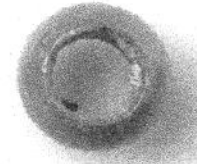 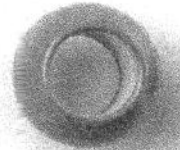 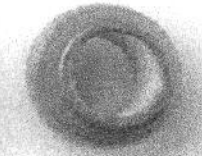

Showing What I Know With KWL Charts and Alternative Assignments

For educators, it makes sense to start a unit by finding out what students know, want to know, and have learned (KWL) once they have taught the unit. Understanding what students know and are interested in before teaching a unit is an excellent way to connect with learners and is a preassessment strategy that is likely familiar to many readers.

Organizing students' prior knowledge in a KWL chart nicely complements this chapter's question 4 strategy of alternative assignments. When students explicitly say they want to learn something, teachers can use that information as a foundation for building learning alternatives for question 4 students to help them excel. At the same time, teachers can gain a better understanding of what struggling students need to review, allowing them to meet the needs of all students.

Preassessment: KWL Charts

We would predict that many of you have completed a KWL chart as a student, used one as a teacher, or have seen one used by a teacher or workshop facilitator. The *KWL chart*, which seeks to find what students know about a topic, what they want to know, and then what they have learned once the teaching begins, has been around since 1986. In an article in *The Reading Teacher*, Donna Ogle (1986) outlines this process as a way to "help honor what children bring to each reading situation and model for their students the importance of accessing appropriate knowledge before reading" (p. 564). While it originated as a reading strategy, the KWL chart can and has been used in teaching any subject area to individuals of any age group.

We have used this as classroom teachers in our work with students and are amazed at how quickly a one-page document can tell educators so much about their class. We have also experienced using this strategy with adults when supporting others who are learning about the Professional Learning Community at Work process. When beginning the day's work with large groups of teachers, we have found this to be a helpful tool to determine what the group collectively already understands and wants to learn more about. If a group, for example, has done a great deal of work around establishing essential outcomes, the leader wouldn't need to spend as much time on that area and could instead focus more time and support in another area, perhaps the area where many in the group have stated they want to learn more. This same principle works in the classroom.

With a simple three-column, one-page document, your team can gain a quick glimpse into what the learners in the room already know and where they have an interest. If students don't know much about the topic, this will be evident in the responses. For students whose responses show a clear understanding of the topic, teachers can follow up to determine which of the standards about to be covered they can consider mastered and which could be mastered in a fraction of the time required by other students (Academic Success Center, 2019).

To support this conversation, we developed what we call the WQA format: asking students *w*hat they would like to learn more about, what *q*uestions they have, and their ideas on potential *a*lternative assignments. This makes sense to us as a strategy to increase student agency and to personalize student learning. By asking these questions, you are tapping into a powerful student-centered instructional strategy because students have an opportunity to own their learning. Here are the steps we recommend for KWL charts supported by the WQA format.

1. Develop a summary statement that would provide an overall glimpse into what students will be learning in this unit.
2. Use the KWL chart provided in figure 3.1 (the reproducible version appears on page 56) as a student handout. For column K, ask students to brainstorm the key words, ideas, phrases, events, and prior knowledge for column K. For column W, ask students to share things that they are interested to know more about. This should last until students have exhausted all of their ideas, typically about five to ten minutes. Explain to students that they will complete column L as they learn more about the unit. Collect all student work.

Unit: ______________ Name: ______________

K: What You Already Know	W: What You Want to Learn More About	L: What You Have Learned in This Unit

Figure 3.1: KWL chart.

3. Once team members have administered the preassessment, they should bring their student-completed documents to the upcoming collaborative team meeting.
4. Team members quickly sort the student responses into three piles: (1) little to no prior knowledge, (2) some prior knowledge, and (3) a high level of prior knowledge.
5. Team members examine the students who demonstrated a high level of prior understanding and create a question 4 stack for students who might qualify for question 4 support for this unit. Individual teachers will want to conduct a one-on-one follow-up with students to learn more about their understanding of this topic.
6. Teachers who have determined question 4 students for this unit will begin to implement the WQA process with students.
7. Near the conclusion of the unit, for all students, redistribute the KWL charts from the first day. Ask students to complete the L column—what they have learned in this unit. This will provide a good overview of what

the students have learned and what concepts might need further review prior to an assessment.

As a result of the KWL preassessment, each teacher should have a good understanding of what individual students have demonstrated knowledge of the content that the unit will cover.

Question 4 Strategy: Alternative Assignments

As with some of the other question 4 strategies, we believe that teachers should confirm student understanding with a brief follow-up discussion. This follow-up will not only provide the teacher with more proof that the student knows the subject matter (which is the top priority), but it will also help the teacher see what the student wants to learn and what questions the student may have. We recommend that teachers gain an awareness of what students have claimed they want to learn from the KWL preassessment and use that information as a foundation for setting up learning alternatives for the qualifying student. This conversation, coupled with what they shared on their preassessment, provides the students with voice and potential choice for their alternative assignment.

The WQA format is key to supporting these conversations with students. Tom Sherrington (2019) shares when advocating this kind of learning opportunity:

> You only have to reflect on your own education to consider when, as a teenager growing up, you started to form legitimate academic interests and preferences; you started asking questions that you wanted answers to; you felt ready to make choices about what to study. (pp. 79–80)

This is not a process that you would undertake for every unit and for every student, but we do believe that it fits well with the KWL preassessment strategy for the students who clearly understand the unit of study. In *Edutopia*'s article highlighting the year 2020's most important educational research findings, it's noted that age-old strategies like highlighting, rereading, and underlining are not nearly as effective as having students develop questions about the content and what they are to learn (Terada & Merrill, 2020). The research base supporting these assertions also makes it clear that the teacher needs to be involved in these processes, supporting and guiding the students along the way in order to ensure that the student is headed in the direction that the teacher and student agreed on (Terada & Merrill, 2020).

If your question 4 students or your teacher team are having trouble determining what would be the best alternative assignment for the unit, we have developed the WQA chart in figure 3.2 (see reproducible version on page 57) to help students process and work with their teacher to determine the best course of action. At the bottom of the WQA chart, the teacher team provides the students with a bank of possible options to consider if they are not able to come up with some of their own ideas. This bank can be added to each year as the teacher team will learn and get ideas from question 4 students on an annual basis.

W: What do you want to learn more about?	Q: What questions do you have about this unit's content?	A: What alternative assignments would help you learn more or answer your questions?
Learning Bank	Question Bank	Alternat ve Assignment Bank

Figure 3.2: WQA chart template.

Using the WQA form, follow these steps.

1. The grade-level or content-area team should brainstorm ideas for the three banks on the WQA form. For primary learners, you may want to consider providing the students with the banks to support them. For intermediate and secondary learners, you may want to consider not providing them initially with any bank items and only have them on hand if the student struggles to answer the questions.

2. Meet with your question 4 students and hand out the WQA form. Provide them with time to complete it. For students unsure of how to answer questions in the columns, ask the following probing questions to get them started.

   W: What do you want to learn more about?

   - Is there something that you are particularly interested in?
   - If you could study one concept or item from this unit, what would it be?
   - What parts weren't interesting to you at all?

   Q: What questions do you have about this unit's content?

   - As you look ahead in this unit, is there something that doesn't seem to make sense?
   - What items are you curious about?

   A: What alternative assignments would help you learn more or answer your questions?

   - If you did a different assignment for this unit, what would it be?
   - From a list of possible choices, which of these final products are most appealing to you? (Easton, n.d.)

3. Collect the WQA form and determine if there are any commonalities among students with their responses. If there are, consider grouping students to work on their alternative assignments in pairs or small groups.
4. After assessing the WQA forms, meet individually or in small groups with students to finalize their questions they want to learn about and how the learning will be assessed with an alternative assignment.
5. During times that make sense during whole-class instruction, allow for students to work, individually or in teams, on the final products you had agreed to when reviewing the completed WQA forms.

Example 1: Fourth-Grade Mathematics

Prior to a fourth-grade collaborative teacher team beginning a mathematics unit on fractions, members discuss and come to an agreement on the learning progressions they will develop for students to demonstrate what they know and can do for this unit and over the course of the year. By having an understanding of what students who are struggling might need to go back to learn and what students who are excelling might be able to learn to move forward, teachers are better equipped to meet the needs of all learners. The teacher team also plans the interventions, common pre- and post-assessments, and an overall learning plan for the upcoming unit.

On the first day of the lessons, each teacher provides sample problems at the front of the room as a bell-ringer activity. From working on these problems, students will have an understanding of the types of problems they will be able to solve at the end of the unit. Students then receive a KWL chart and teachers ask them to complete the K and the W columns to show what they already know and what they want to learn more about. Teachers also let the students know that if they think they can solve any of the problems on the board, they should go for it in the K column.

Once the collaborative team members have a chance to review which students they determine already know the material, teachers meet with this extension team in the classroom and make them their own individual small group. Each day of the class during mathematics block after whole-group instruction, the teacher starts with this team and offers new and different problems for the team to solve, which are more challenging than the problems being considered by the rest of the class. The challenging problems could come from those the collaborative team developed for this specific purpose or even units that will ultimately be a part of the fifth-grade learning progressions.

A regular routine for the teacher working with the students on these teams would be to discuss what they learned in the whole group and then push toward challenging problems they might find interesting. The teacher continually offers ideas to the students by saying things such as, "I have this interesting problem you might like. Would your team want to take a shot at solving it?" By completing this routine with each mathematics unit during the year, the students who need to be challenged the most received those opportunities.

Example 2: Ninth-Grade Physical Science

A ninth-grade physical science team works together to prepare a unit that focuses on standards and indicators related to motion and forces. With this focus, the team spends a lot of time teaching about and providing experiences related to Newton's three laws of motion.

The team is excited about this unit because it seems like a perfect representation of what education author and professor Jo Boaler (n.d.) calls a "low floor and high ceiling" activity. Every student can access and complete the activity, and those who want can soar and take it as far as they want. This activity is perfectly aligned to the idea of challenging students who already know the material.

To begin the unit, the team shares a quick video compilation of some of the activities that students will complete during the course of the unit. After watching the video, the teachers supply the students with a KWL chart, asking them what they already know about this material and what they want to know more about. By seeing which students have some background or passion for this area, they learn who they could challenge and offer ideas to push beyond what they would typically expect. This chart, along with the inventories taken at the start of the year, allowed the teachers to really know the students and how they feel about science, how they feel when they are engaged in learning, and what it's like when they get to feel smart in class.

As an introduction to the concept of force and Newton's laws, students are assigned to teams of two; they receive an assignment to find a toy around the house that moves, and use it to analyze how force interacts with the toy. The idea that you really know a topic when you teach it to someone else comes to life when the ninth-grade students, once the first part of the assignment was completed, walk down the street to a neighboring elementary school. While there, the students taught the concepts using the toys to a group of fourth-grade students, who then evaluate the older students on creativity and design. Even the most struggling learners stepped up to the plate to shine when working with the younger students.

Next, the students take part in an activity where they use what they learned about force to design, build, and launch a rocket. The rocket is launched from a two-liter rocket launcher, which launches rockets as far as 160 meters. Every rocket built will be launched; some just go farther. The farthest launches receive awards, and the teachers hang photos of the best launches on the walls of their classrooms to preserve these accomplishments. This activity builds community and really hooks students into learning.

All students are allowed and challenged to be as engaged in this assignment as possible. For those students who are really excited about and know about force and motion, there are many ways to excel through alternative or additional assignments. Students who want to compete are in a position to really require extension. If they want to finish in the top three, students will need to use tools and materials in the woodshop for a lighter rocket and study the data from flights in years past, kept in binders by the teachers, so they can use this information to develop their own rockets.

At the end of the unit, each of the students complete the last column of the KWL chart with what they learned. This is an excellent final representation of what learners of all levels take from the activity as they learn about force and motion.

Chapter Reflection

In chapter 9 (page 127), you will review what you have learned and tried from each chapter to make future planning decisions to determine which strategies will work best for your team. To assist in this, consider the following questions.

Preassessment Reflection Questions: KWL Charts

1. Did this strategy help your team identify question 4 students?
2. Did this strategy take a reasonable amount of teacher time to implement?
3. Did this strategy take a reasonable amount of classroom time to implement?
4. Can you see your team using this strategy for future units to determine which students already know the material?

Question 4 Strategy Reflection Questions: Alternative Assignments

1. Were students able to succeed as a result of this strategy?
2. Was this strategy easy for teachers to use?
3. Was this challenging for students?
4. Was this engaging for students?
5. Can you see your team using this strategy for future units to challenge students who already know the material?

KWL Chart

Unit: ____________________ Name: ____________________

K: What You Already Know	W: What You Want to Learn More About	L: What You Have Learned in This Unit

WQA Chart Template

W: What do you want to learn more about?	Q: What questions do you have about this unit's content?	A: What alternative assignments would help you learn more or answer your questions?
Learning Bank	Question Bank	Alternative Assignment Bank

CHAPTER 4

      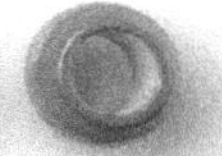

Showing What I Know With Student Questions and Question Formulation

Questioning is a key part of every classroom. Can you imagine how many questions you were personally asked over your K–12 experience? Mark, did you complete your homework last night? Steve, can you share how you solved for *x*? It makes sense, as asking questions serves a fundamental purpose when information is being shared from a teacher to their students. It allows for teachers to find out what students know, learn where gaps are in the students' understanding, and determine what students already know. The use of questions is so important, in fact, it is one of the nine research-based strategies featured in one of the most-read education books of all time, *Classroom Instruction That Works* (Marzano, Pickering, & Pollock, 2001). In this work, the authors suggest using higher-level questions in order to encourage students to analyze information and offer specific strategies that teachers can use when developing these questions.

In this case, for the unit you have selected, you will learn what students know by asking them to develop their own questions. Teams can then use the types of questions that students develop as a form of data for teams to analyze and determine who will be considered a question 4 student. This group of learners will then receive directions to use their questions and be part of a question formulation activity, where the students who show they know this information can work to solve the difficult questions that they or class members have created. In this chapter, we discuss how the question formulation technique allows students the opportunity to learn and explore in their own way to answer the questions they develop during the student questions preassessment.

Preassessment: Student Questions

In this preassessment strategy, we are advocating a shift from teachers asking students the questions to students asking the questions. According to authors Dan Rothstein and Luz Santana (2017), codirectors of the Right Question Institute, when students know how to ask their own questions, they take greater ownership of their learning, deepen comprehension, and make new connections and discoveries on their own. The Right Question Institute (https://rightquestion.org/education), funded by the Library of Congress, offers a variety of tools and resources for teams to support students on how to formulate, work with, and use their own questions. As a teacher using this as a preassessment strategy, you can learn a great deal in a very short amount of time about what a student knows about the content based on the questions they ask.

For example, if a teacher is getting ready to teach a unit on the American Revolution and shares a quick summary of the upcoming unit, student questions would reveal who already might know the content. As leaders of the classroom, teachers seek students who study this topic on their own because it is something that is interesting to them. Low-level questions would be very basic and might come from somebody who is not familiar with the topic at all. The resulting questions might sound like this.

- What is a revolution?
- Who fought whom?
- Why was there a war?
- How recently did this war take place?

While there is nothing wrong with these questions, the one asking them clearly formed them without prior knowledge in this area. Students asking these questions are not likely to trigger you to think that the student is in need of a question 4 strategy.

On the other hand, questions asked by students who do have some prior knowledge might sound like this.

- What kind of a leader would Thomas Jefferson be in today's government?
- What if the Boston Massacre never occurred?
- What current events could you compare to the Boston Tea Party?

A teacher reading these questions is likely to see them as a sign that the student has prior knowledge about this era of history. Perhaps the student has visited Boston or other key historical areas, has a personal interest in this topic, or has learned about this in another class. Coupled with a follow-up conversation with the student, these questions might indicate that a question 4 strategy is warranted.

We recommend learning what students know by asking them to ask questions, which includes the following steps.

1. Develop a summary statement to provide an overall glimpse into what students will learn in this unit.
2. Brainstorm a list of questions students might ask about this unit using figure 4.1 (the reproducible version is on page 72). Consider all possible answers. When you begin to exhaust your list, think of questions you might receive from specific students in your class.
3. With your exhaustive list, select a point value for each question using the following point scale. This document will allow you to quickly sort the student responses at a future collaborative team meeting.

   The question reflects:

   - 0—no prior knowledge
   - 2—some prior knowledge
   - 4—a high level of prior knowledge

Brainstorm Questions Students Might Ask			
Possible Question	**Points (0, 2, or 4)**	**Possible Question**	**Points (0, 2, or 4)**
1		13	
2		14	
3		15	
4		16	
5		17	

Figure 4.1: Collaborative team brainstorming tool for student questions.

continued →

Possible Question	Points (0, 2, or 4)	Possible Question	Points (0, 2, or 4)
6		18	
7		19	
8		20	
9		21	
10		22	
11		23	
12		24	

4. Provide students with the student questions preassessment (figure 4.2, with the reproducible version on page 73) and allow five minutes to complete.

Unit: ________________ Name: ________________

In this next unit, we will be learning:

When looking at what we are about to study, what questions might you have about this topic?

Figure 4.2: Student questions preassessment.

5. Once team members have administered the preassessment, they bring their student-completed preassessments to the upcoming collaborative team meeting.
6. Team members quickly sort the student responses into three piles: (1) little to no prior knowledge, (2) some prior knowledge, and (3) a high level of prior knowledge.
7. Team members examine the piles for students who might be considered question 4 students for this unit. Individual teachers may want to conduct a one-on-one follow-up conversation with students to learn more about their understanding of this topic.

Question 4 Strategy: Question Formulation

Question formulation is an instructional technique that we have seen work well for an entire classroom with all learners. Its use does not need to be limited to students who might be considered question 4 students. We do see it as a type of extension activity that teachers could use with students who demonstrate understanding of the subject matter during the student question preassessment. The question formulation technique is a step-by-step process designed to facilitate students asking questions; those questions then serve as the starting point for instruction, assessment, or a future project. Many teachers who use this method share that it is a powerful tool for increasing student engagement and collaboration.

The question formulation process starts with teachers designing a focus for the lesson using some form of a statement or an image to attract student attention. Next, students produce questions in a structured format for open-ended thinking. Students then improve their questions by considering the differences between open- and closed-ended questions. Once questions are modified to be open ended, students prioritize the questions and then the students and teacher decide together on how students will demonstrate learning. The last step is completed when students reflect on what they learned (Perkins, 2020; Rothstein & Santana, 2017).

The fourth step in question formulation is really where the question 4 students receive opportunities for extension. When students prioritize their questions, they begin to group the questions that were asked and identify those that are the most interesting to explore further. In classrooms where we have visited, teachers may choose three or four questions for the class and ask students to pick the question that is most interesting to them. Once students determine those areas of interest, they determine how they are going to answer the question and what tools they might use to be able to do so. In many ways, this reminds us of opportunities like Genius Hour (the popular Google program to spend a percentage of company time on personal projects that many teachers have adapted for the classroom) and the Schoolwide Enrichment Model (Renzulli & Reis, 2014) that really seek to better understand students' passions and interests by providing voice and choice in their learning. This is a very structured way for content-area instructors to offer a form of personalized learning.

We recommend the following steps for using the generated questions.

1. Bring together the students who were considered question 4 students after reviewing the preassessment and have follow-up conversations. These students will have the opportunity to work together during this unit of instruction. In some settings, this might mean students from multiple classes coming to one area to work together. In other settings, it might mean a small group of students in one class collaborating. In groups, students determine who will assume which roles. Figure 4.3 (see the reproducible version on page 74) provides a tool to help choose roles.

ROLES TO ASSIGN

- **Facilitator:** Moderates team discussion, keeps the group on task, and distributes work
- **Recorder:** Keeps notes on team discussions
- **Presenter:** Serves as the spokesperson to the class or instructor, summarizing the group's activities and conclusions
- **Timekeeper:** Keeps the group aware of time constraints and deadlines and makes sure meetings start on time
- **Awesome team member:** Whether or not they are assigned a specific role, all members of the team will work together to demonstrate their learning in this unit

MEMBERS ASSIGNED

- Facilitator:
- Recorder:
- Presenter:
- Timekeeper:
- Awesome team members:

Figure 4.3: Team roles for student questions.

2. Provide students the opportunity to review each other's questions, and ask the group to develop a group list, using an organizer like figure 4.4 (see reproducible version on page 75). The new list should have no duplicate questions. Students work together to convert any closed questions to open-ended questions.

Questions	Open or Closed	Question Changed to Open (If Needed)	Spend a Buck

Figure 4.4: Student questions handout.

3. With the final list of questions, teachers ask students to hypothetically spend a buck. If students had a dollar to spend on any of the questions they found most interesting or compelling, how would they spend it? All the votes could go to one question or be divided equally among different questions. Students would be in full control over how they want to spend their "money."

4. Students analyze the voting and note the questions that were most interesting to the group.
5. Students choose two to four questions with the most votes, and select an interest area. Student teams then determine a game plan for answering the compelling question they have chosen. Also, as part of this conversation, students determine how they will demonstrate this learning. This could include a presentation, video, collage, drawing, story, infographic, poster, podcast, or digital portfolio.
6. Students receive time to work with their question 4 groups to solve the questions they have developed throughout the unit.
7. Students present their answers to the teacher and class at the end of the unit.
8. Students develop a reflection document for the teacher on what they learned, how they solved the problem, and how they interacted with their teammates.

Use the student directions handout in figure 4.5 (see reproducible version on page 76) to facilitate these steps.

1. On the student questions team roles handout, determine roles for members of your team. Depending on the size of your group, participants may need to serve in multiple roles: facilitator, recorder, presenter, timekeeper, or awesome team member.
2. On the student questions handout, complete column 1. Without repeating questions, list all the questions each individual developed.
3. In column 2, with each question, determine if it is an open or closed question. Open-ended questions are those that don't have a specific yes-or-no answer and can encourage new questions. Closed questions are those that have specific answers.
4. In column 3, for those questions that are closed, alter the wording to make them open ended.
5. In column 4, team members each determine how they would spend a dollar on each of the questions based on the question that is most interesting to them. If one member wants to spend 100 cents on one item and none on the other, 33 cents on three different items, or any other arrangement, this works just fine.
6. Determine the two to four questions that seem the most interesting to the group.
7. Choose one of the questions you would like to solve.

8. Work together to answer the question you have chosen. The person assigned to be the presenter shares the team's chosen question and initial thoughts for how this learning will be demonstrated at the end of the unit.
9. At the conclusion of the unit, team members each write a one- to two-page document highlighting what you learned, how you solved the problem, and how you interacted with your teammates.

Figure 4.5: Directions for student questions.

Example 1: Fifth Grade

A collaborative team made up of fifth-grade teachers asks the school counselor to join the team to talk about how to better help students who appear to be struggling and having a hard time managing their emotions and their interactions with peers. As they talk more about this and the trends they have seen in recent years, team members decide that this is an important concept and that they will pay special attention to the social-emotional learning of all their students. While the district doesn't have a set curriculum in place, they decide that they will address the emotional needs of their students on their own during morning class time. Through their conversations, they begin to call this work *good-person curriculum*.

They see over and over that students need help in controlling their emotions when they face adversity in frustrating social situations. The teachers look at various social-emotional learning curricula and standards provided on the internet and talk through what they feel all students should know and be able to do in this area. They settle on *emotion management*—being able to calm down, manage anxiety, and handle negative words from friends—as a key place to start.

As they talk about emotion management, they also recognize that all students have different needs and acknowledge that they aren't sure how to begin their work. One of the teachers has just received professional learning about using the question formulation technique in her science class; she shares that this could be an excellent way to approach this social-emotional learning unit as well.

The team decides to develop its unit around the use of questioning. First, the teachers share a short podcast about emotions that they found on the internet. Sports have been a frequent rallying point for the students in their classrooms or homerooms, so they enjoyed hearing about emotions and what stress does to a person's biological systems. There is a reason that athletes perform better until being subjected to stress, and that then their performance suffers. The key point from the podcast was about how emotions really affect people, and by relating it to sports, teachers were able to really drive it home.

Teachers then ask the students to create questions based on this podcast and think about what made them curious. Once the list of questions was on the board, teachers give a short minilesson on how to make questions open ended and thought provoking, as opposed to those that could be answered with a yes, no, or short answer (that is, closed). After this lesson, students receive an opportunity to revise their work.

With the podcast and thought-provoking questions in mind, the teachers give students a short self-assessment about handling one's emotions. Over the course of the week, the teachers work with students at a convenient time for both to talk about what they had learned so far in the social-emotional learning lesson and to go over their self-assessment. As a team, the teacher and student then talk about areas where the student can most improve and the question that the class developed that might be the best to research an answer. At times, the teacher can also expertly match certain students together for group projects.

Teachers push and challenge students who seem to excel at managing their emotions as reflected on the self-assessment to take on questions that focus on how to be leaders in situations when others are struggling with emotions. Students in the extension group who were already proficient at this skill would then go back through and develop new questions around this leadership idea.

All students in the class, including the student leadership team members who demonstrated proficiency, work together by researching and developing answers to their questions. At the end of the unit, each student group, including those the teacher created and the extension group with the leadership theme, presents its findings. The teachers report that this intentional and deliberate approach to answering the questions they have formulated for themselves has played a major role in advancing the community of their classroom.

Example 2: Tenth-Grade American History

A tenth-grade American history team works together to put a new focus on the last unit of the year, which is the Civil War. Since the school is located in the eastern part of the United States, this is an area where many students in the classroom already have an interest. Each year, team members reflect on the fact that, during this unit, many students either become bored or assume the role of teacher helpers. The teachers think they can do more to push and challenge their students.

The teachers decide that they will learn what students know by asking them what questions they have about the Civil War before they even introduce the topic. The teachers brainstorm various questions that students might develop. Then they assign a point value (0, 2, or 4) to the various questions to represent the level of understanding they think would be required from each of the students to ask that question. For example, What is the Civil War?, How did the North win the Civil War?, and What played more of a role in the beginning of the Civil War, slavery or sectionalism, and why? demonstrate distinct levels of prior knowledge. These three questions might show which students are fully novices, which ones have some understanding, and which ones show a great deal of understanding. The team members share that they can get a good idea of what students know about the subject based on the thinking that goes into their questions.

After the students complete the previous unit's test, they receive a blank document and the task to write down any questions they have about the Civil War. The teachers review the questions and can quickly see who is just learning about this topic and who really has a strong working knowledge.

On the first full day of the unit, the teachers greet the students and direct them to stations all over the room. They ask students to attend at least four stations of their choice and answer the questions located at each one. Stations include battle-in-a-box diorama assignments that students had created in past years, video clips of scenes from Civil War films, maps, board games, and biographies of individuals during this time, which could include soldiers, politicians, women, slaves, and Indigenous people, for example. Each of the stations has various challenges that range in level, where students with prior knowledge can answer extension questions. Engagement is high as students carefully make their way around the stations.

After the stations, teachers ask the students, as a class, to develop new questions they now might have about the Civil War. After looking at the class list of questions, it is easy to see that their interest level has been piqued and that students could frame the questions in a different way to help support future activities. Teachers conduct a quick minilesson on how to ask open-ended questions and ask the students to go back and reword the questions in order to invite responses beyond yes, no, or a quick answer. The questions, as the teacher explains, need to be thought provoking and often lead to new questions.

After this activity, teachers lead an activity in which the class works to prioritize the questions based on interest level and narrow them down to four that are the most interesting to them: (1) Why was the war fought in the first place? (2) Why did President Lincoln age so much in a short amount of time? (3) How many people died in the war? and (4) Could the desired effect of the war have been achieved in a way other than fighting? Once the class settles on four key questions, teachers tell them to choose their team to investigate and solve the questions they had chosen. During the selection of questions, teachers pull the extension students aside and ask if they would want to take on a more challenging task. Once the extension group is in agreement, teachers choose the most challenging and thought-provoking questions that these students formed from the preassessment. With these questions, the extension group members do some rewording and choose the one that was most interesting to them. The extension team discusses a question that would connect with world events. They decide that it will be really interesting and engaging to answer the question, When considering the Civil War, how is the present embedded in the past and how is the past embedded in the present? While everyone in the class is working on a question, this complex question is the most challenging. The teachers expertly work the students' answers and class presentations into the flow of the unit as they learn about the Civil War.

Chapter Reflection

In chapter 9 (page 127), you will review what you have learned and tried from each chapter to make future planning decisions to determine which strategies will work best for your team. To assist in this, consider the following questions.

Preassessment Reflection Questions: Student Questions

1. Did this strategy help your team identify question 4 students?
2. Did this strategy take a reasonable amount of teacher time to implement?
3. Did this strategy take a reasonable amount of classroom time to implement?
4. Can you see your team using this strategy for future units to determine which students already know the material?

Question 4 Strategy Reflection Questions: Question Formulation

1. Were students able to succeed as a result of this strategy?
2. Was this strategy easy for teachers to use?
3. Was this challenging for students?
4. Was this engaging for students?
5. Can you see your team using this strategy for future units to challenge students who already know the material?

Collaborative Team Brainstorming Tool for Student Questions

Brainstorm Questions Students Might Ask			
Possible Question	Points (0, 2, or 4)	Possible Question	Points (0, 2, or 4)
1		13	
2		14	
3		15	
4		16	
5		17	
6		18	
7		19	
8		20	
9		21	
10		22	
11		23	
12		24	

Student Questions Preassessment

Unit: ______________________ Name: ______________________

In this next unit, we will be learning:

When looking at what we are about to study, what questions might you have about this topic?

Team Roles for Student Questions

ROLES TO ASSIGN

- **Facilitator:** Moderates team discussion, keeps the group on task, and distributes work
- **Recorder:** Keeps notes on team discussions, the group's activities, and conclusions
- **Presenter:** Serves as the spokesperson to the class or instructor, summarizing the group's activities and conclusions
- **Timekeeper:** Keeps the group aware of time constraints and deadlines and makes sure meetings start on time
- **Awesome team member:** Whether or not they are assigned a specific role, all members of the team will work together to demonstrate their learning in this unit

MEMBERS ASSIGNED

- Facilitator:
- Recorder:
- Presenter:
- Timekeeper:
- Awesome team members:

Student Questions Handout

Questions	Open or Closed	Question Changed to Open (If Needed)	Spend a Buck

Directions for Student Questions

1. On the student questions team roles handout, determine roles for members of your team. Depending on the size of your group, participants may need to serve in multiple roles: facilitator, recorder, presenter, timekeeper, or awesome team member.
2. On the student questions handout, complete column 1. Without repeating questions, list all the questions each individual developed.
3. In column 2, with each question, determine if it is an open or closed question. Open-ended questions are those that don't have a specific yes-or-no answer and can encourage new questions. Closed questions are those that have specific answers.
4. In column 3, for those questions that are closed, alter the wording to make them open ended.
5. In column 4, team members each determine how they would spend a dollar on each of the questions based on the question that is most interesting to them. If one member wants to spend 100 cents on one item and none on the other, 33 cents on three different items, or any other arrangement, this works just fine.
6. Determine the two to four questions that seem the most interesting to the group.
7. Choose one of the questions you would like to solve.
8. Work together to answer the question you have chosen. The person assigned to be the presenter shares the team's chosen question and initial thoughts for how this learning will be demonstrated at the end of the unit.
9. At the conclusion of the unit, team members each write a one- to two-page document highlighting what you learned, how you solved the problem, and how you interacted with your teammates.

CHAPTER 5

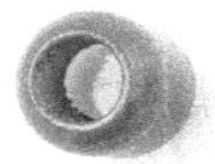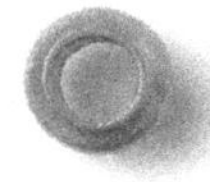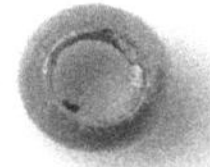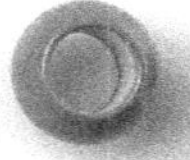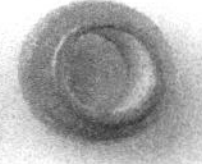

Showing What I Know With Drawing and Badges

We can hardly think of a less threatening activity in a classroom, kindergarten through senior year, than asking students to draw a picture. Our minds immediately go to the primary grades, where we drew for pleasure, often whatever we wanted. We think of the middle grades (sixth through eighth) where our two respective schools must have gone to the same workshop hundreds of miles away because we both remember consistently using interactive notebooks in social studies and science. Ironically, we both remember using them at the start of the school years, until interactive notebook fatigue began, and our teachers got tired of checking the notebooks on a frequent basis. For those who didn't use interactive notebooks, it's simply a process where you write your notes about the most relevant information the teacher shares on the left-hand side of each page and use the right-hand side for images and drawings to help you connect with what the teacher said at a later time. To be honest, we really don't remember drawing much of anything in high school other than diagrams of things that were dissected in science class.

Drawing is a powerful activity that can engage students' brains in different ways than activities that involve writing words. The same is true of badges, which offer a way to motivate and reward students. This chapter discusses these two strategies.

Preassessment: Drawing

Asking students to draw, in general, is an activity that teachers of all grade levels can use. Research analyst Youki Terada (2019) writes:

> So when we draw, we encode the memory in a very rich way, layering together the visual memory of the image, and the semantic memory that is invoked when we engage in meaning-making. In combination, this greatly increases the likelihood that the concept being drawn will later be recalled.

In one study, participants were asked to either write or draw key words they had just studied. Later, they remembered twice as many of the words from the list they had drawn. Drawing was found to be a reliable and easily replicable means of boosting performance and memory (Fernandes, Wammes, & Meade, 2018).

These results make sense. Drawing requires learners to interpret what they know about what they have learned. Students can't just copy words from pages or just repeat back what they have heard someone say. This connects with research on the topic of whether teachers and college professors should allow note taking on laptops. While a laptop would seem to have its advantages, the practice of note taking freehand and actively making drawings and images to demonstrate learning is a far better way to synthesize and summarize information for a learner (Diemand-Yauman, Oppenheimer, & Vaughan, 2010).

When determining a technique to learn what students already know about the content, using a familiar, safe, and proven approach like drawing to help students with recall certainly seems like a valuable common assessment strategy to use at the start of the unit. Here are the steps we recommend.

1. Using the standards and indicators for the upcoming course, determine the three most essential concepts you will be teaching in the unit.
2. For each of these items, determine the type of images that would demonstrate to your team that students have a clear understanding of this topic.
3. Determine what your team will use as evidence that a student knows the material.
4. Determine the prompt you would use to influence students to develop the desired images. Looking at your unit, what will you ask students to draw? Use figure 5.1 to facilitate these steps. Then you can use the student handout in figure 5.2 to administer the preassessment. Reproducible versions of both tools appear on pages 87 and 88.

Most Essential Concepts to Be Covered	Image or Creation That Would Demonstrate the Student Understands This Concept	Types of Evidence the Student Understands the Material	Prompt to Provide to Students
1.			
2.			
3.			

Figure 5.1: Planning guide for student drawing.

For each of the following essential concepts, draw an image that explains what you already know about this topic. If you are not familiar at all with what we are about to study, this is fine; you aren't expected to. Feel free to leave it blank or draw a picture of something else you like. Don't be too detailed. This shouldn't take more than ten minutes.
Prompt 1:
Prompt 2:
Prompt 3:

Figure 5.2: Student drawing handout.

Question 4 Strategy: Badges

The use of badges in the electronic world has become quite widespread. Many games that people play electronically have some sort of badging component to them. If you are not familiar with this concept, we would encourage you to ask your students or your own children about how they get recognition for achievements in the latest video game they are playing on their game system or phone. Educational program designer Nora Priest (2016) defines a *digital badge* as "an online validation of an achievement, skill, or credential" (p. 5). Digital badges, also referred to as *micro-credentials*, can be part of a larger digital portfolio, are popular in many arenas, and have begun to emerge more and more in mainstream education. We have personally seen digital badges increase in popularity in recent years in the education field in professional learning for teachers. As an example, if your school district uses Google products, it's likely that you have had the opportunity to get certified as a level 1 or level 2 Google Educator. In order to get this recognition, you have to complete a series of modules and then take a test to get your certification. When you are officially certified, you receive a simple Google icon that you can attach to your email signature to let everyone know that you indeed are a recognized Google Educator.

With that basic understanding, the strategy that we are advocating is to create badges for your students that provide proper validation for demonstrating mastery of an expected learning standard. The badges could be digital as we already described, or you can also use a wide range of physical badges. Physical badges could be stickers, buttons, small signs, patches, or tags. The physical and electronic badge options are essentially limitless; what matters is that they offer a form of recognition that acknowledges that something was learned or mastered. Why are we encouraging this as a strategy? Priest (2016) shares that research indicates the following potential benefits of creating badging experiences with students.

- They give students formative feedback about whether they have achieved learning criteria.
- They provide students greater autonomy.
- They allow students to better demonstrate their learning.
- They improve student motivation.

We would like to note that the research findings shared by Priest are all aligned with the outcomes that we seek with a quality personalized learning environment for students.

David Niguidula (2019), education consultant and proponent of badges and digital portfolios, has developed criteria for how teachers might deem student assignments as portfolio worthy. We believe that teams can apply these criteria during their consideration of badging assignments and activities. Niguidula's (2019) criteria are as follows.

- The assignment should require effort.
- The assignment should allow for some level of student voice and choice.
- The assignment should be authentic to the subject area.
- The assignment should require the application of knowledge.
- The assignment should generate a product that students would be proud to display.

The badge process can be as simple or as complicated as the team wants to make it. Digital badges have no cost, but creating them does require some work. As classrooms become more and more digital, you can attach badges to your electronic classroom, student email signatures, and even learning platforms. Conversely, depending on what the team decides, physical badges may have a cost attached to them (such as buying tags, stickers, patches, and so on), but you may be able to create them at little to no cost with school supplies. Students might display physical badges in the classroom, on folders and lockers, and even on backpacks or personal items. We highly encourage that the teacher team creates badges that are age appropriate and that students would be proud to have. We recommend the following steps for badges.

1. Based on the drawing preassessment, determine which students will be considered question 4 students for the current unit.
2. Based on the standards, create badges or badge levels for different skills or proficiency attainments. Use the badge creation document (figure 5.3) to assist your team in this process. The reproducible version is available on page 89.

Standard or Standards	Type of Badge	Badge Level	Skill or Proficiency Expected

Figure 5.3: Badge creation document.

3. Determine how badges will correlate to a grade if necessary.
4. Share the badge goal sheet in figure 5.4 (see reproducible version on page 90) with your students and engage the question 4 students in it.

Name: ________________________

1. What badge standard (or learning pathway) will you be pursuing?
2. What badge level will you be pursuing? Why does this level interest you?
3. How will you demonstrate your proficiency?

Figure 5.4: Badge goal sheet.

Example 1: Eighth-Grade English

An eighth-grade English team discovers that, each year, the teachers end a major unit about eight to nine days before spring break. They have always struggled with determining whether they would start the next major unit, have it cut in the middle with a week off, and then continue. During their collaborative team time, they determine that they want to develop a short-story unit that would emphasize the importance of communication through storytelling, listening, speaking, reading, writing, and higher-order thinking skills. As the teachers begin the unit, they determine three stories they want all students to read, with an extra three for students who wanted to have their learning extended. They also work together to make the unit into a game that revolves around earning badges.

The teacher team determines that there are two ways to determine which students already know the material and who process the information more deeply and quickly than the others. For the first component, they give the students a form with the names of five stories (and a blank row for a sixth story) on the left-hand column of the paper and a black space on the right. Not all students will get to the sixth story. They ask the students to draw a quick image of what they know about the story or what they expect to learn about it. This short activity shows the teachers who already knows the story and creates a hook for the students as they think about what the title might mean. Students who already know the story can do an alternative assignment.

Students who already know the story receive an alternate story to read, provided they haven't read that one as well. If they had read this one as well, the teacher can draw from a list of alternatives. After this, it is time to share the lesson with the student. The title of the unit is "Ready Reader One," a play on the book and movie *Ready Player One*, which is about a person stuck inside a video game who must pass through different worlds to get back to the normal world. For this unit in English class, each story represents a world that the students must escape. When they pass through a world, they earn a badge by completing a series of assignments, including tasks like grammar, vocabulary, and comprehension quizzes, that students can complete at their own pace. Also, each world has chance cards students can draw before the student moves on to the next world. Chance cards consist of items like critical-thinking questions that connect the story to current events. For taking on and completing a chance card, students earn classroom bucks that they can redeem for things like school-themed pencils and other rewards, such as the ability to bring food or a comfort object, like a blanket, to class. The chance cards are ridiculously popular and represent yet another way to challenge students who know the material very quickly.

When students finish each world, they can engage in a "boss battle," which rewards a golden badge for victory. Each boss battle is a contest that acts as an exit ticket from the world they just left; in practice, it's a short activity tied to what they just read. These don't take very long to complete, but they capture the students' attention and become a big motivator. The boss battle for a story about a grandmaster chess player, for example, allows students to play a game of chess (if they know how) or checkers. A story about a race is topped off by a race to get rid of cards in a card game similar to Uno.

Each student is required to earn at least three badges. Students who want extension can go through all five worlds and gain admittance to the secret sixth world (the blank row on the preassessment form, which can now be filled in). A perfect score is six golden badges, which confers the highest classroom honor and earns students a spot on the Ready Reader One wall in the classroom. At the end of the unit, teachers hold a fun awards ceremony where they give out various awards. While the most chance cards, most badges, and most boss battle victories are recognized, so are the hardest workers, the biggest comeback, and the best team players.

Students who need to be challenged are considered in so many different ways in this activity. The teachers check to see which students know the stories, challenge students to complete more than the minimum number of stories, and provide chance cards for more challenging activities. This unit represents an example of an activity in which all students could participate and others could push the learning further.

Example 2: High School Geometry

A high school geometry team that teaches students from varying grade levels but focuses mostly on sophomores works together to determine the best possible learning plan to teach measuring and calculating solids, surface area, and volume. In the three-week-long unit, team members determine that there are seven key concepts that are critical for all students to understand and demonstrate. In addition, they want to give the unit flexible pacing, meaning that they can pace it traditionally or faster depending on the knowledge students have when they enter the classroom or in the time it takes the students to learn.

In the introduction of the unit, students receive an outline of a traditional pacing guide that covers the fifteen planned days of the unit, with the key concepts and entrance tickets clearly marked. The seven key concepts are each tagged with an electronic badge containing a URL or QR code for students to access on their personal devices; each student will need to earn all seven badges before moving to the next unit.

Students who want a traditional experience can show up to class each day knowing what to expect and the topics that the teacher would cover. After learning about the concept, they would take a short formative assessment, which would serve as an entrance ticket to begin work on the next key concept. Once they earn that entrance ticket, they also earn a badge. Each student's progress toward the badges appears on the class website. Students are able to submit their assignment to the teacher, who in turn triggers the earned badge designation.

It is important to note that each entrance ticket requires the students to draw or build something to demonstrate what they have learned in the prior lesson. A typical example of this is the use of paper nets, which are basically regular pieces of paper with directions for students to shape and fold in certain ways and then answer questions. In this case, these questions are based on geometry questions that prove that the students understand the material from the current chapter in their student textbook. By creating these paper nets and answering a few key questions, the teacher can determine progress.

For students wanting to excel at a faster rate and to get additional badges beyond the required seven, the teachers put other mechanisms into place. Each of the lessons had been prerecorded from a prior year. The students could follow the class or watch the prerecorded videos of the lessons from prior years on their own and move forward. Some students use class time to move through up to three concepts in one day. With each concept, the student cannot progress without demonstrating that they know and understand the previous concept.

When students move through the concepts and take the assessment, there are times where they don't know it as well as they thought. When this happens, they could go back and view the video again, seek out the teacher for one-to-one support, or rejoin the larger class. After completing one or more of these, they again attempt the entrance ticket assessment. These entrance tickets truly show where students are in their quest to earn badges and complete the full unit.

The final assessment at the end of the three weeks looks very familiar to all students, as it is in the same configuration as the traditional questions that accompanied the entrance tickets during the unit. However, because students are working at their own pace, there are additional badges to be earned for those who work more quickly through the unit. These students can earn an additional eighth badge or extension by demonstrating the concepts of surface area, lateral area, volume, and density with their own creation. Instead of a canned assignment to use a variety of solids to create a model and demonstrate the space, area, and volume using paper nets, students can use anything from their imagination.

In this class, students who know the material or grasp the concepts quickly use their time in class once they master the seven concepts to take part in activities that are engaging and motivating to them. Student extension activities might include creating a video game to demonstrate elements of the project, digitally building planes and tanks and showing the key measurements on these items, welding various objects, or creating a clown out of shapes off a 3-D printer. Each of these tasks requires students to demonstrate key ideas and terms from the class on their final projects. As the teachers share the eight badge products as they are completed, it is evident that students are trying to outperform the other classes. The engagement and excitement of the class for learning geometry is not something that would have occurred without this extension.

Chapter Reflection

In chapter 9 (page 127), you will review what you have learned and tried from each chapter to make future planning decisions to determine which strategies will work best for your team. To assist in this, consider the following questions.

Preassessment Reflection Questions: Drawing

1. Did this strategy help your team identify question 4 students?
2. Did this strategy take a reasonable amount of teacher time to implement?

3. Did this strategy take a reasonable amount of classroom time to implement?
4. Can you see your team using this strategy for future units to determine which students already know the material?

Question 4 Strategy Reflection Questions: Badges

1. Were students able to succeed as a result of this strategy?
2. Was this strategy easy for teachers to use?
3. Was this challenging for students?
4. Was this engaging for students?
5. Can you see your team using this strategy for future units to challenge students who already know the material?

Planning Guide for Student Drawing

Most Essential Concepts to Be Covered	Image or Creation That Would Demonstrate the Student Understands This Concept	Types of Evidence the Student Understands the Material	Prompt to Provide to Students
1.			
2.			
3.			

Student Drawing Handout

For each of the following essential concepts, draw an image that explains what you already know about this topic. If you are not familiar at all with what we are about to study, this is fine; you aren't expected to. Feel free to leave it blank or draw a picture of something else you like. Don't be too detailed. This shouldn't take more than ten minutes.
Prompt 1:
Prompt 2:
Prompt 3:

Badge Creation Document

Standard or Standards	Type of Badge	Badge Level	Skill or Proficiency Expected

Badge Goal Sheet

Name: ______________________

1. What badge standard (or learning pathway) will you be pursuing?

2. What badge level will you be pursuing? Why does this level interest you?

3. How will you demonstrate your proficiency?

CHAPTER 6

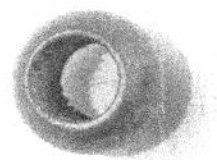 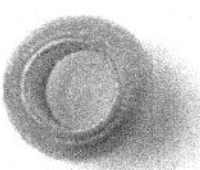 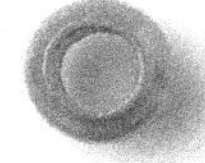  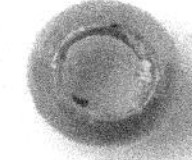 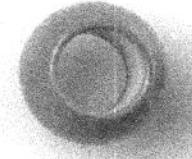 

Showing What I Know With Skimming and Gaming

As a fourth-grade student, coauthor Mark was crazy about sports. As a birthday present, his parents ordered the magazine *Sports Illustrated* for him to keep up with his zest for sports and to encourage him to practice reading. It worked. Every Thursday, Mark would come home from school to check the mail for his weekly delivery of the magazine. Each week, he would thumb through the magazine looking at the table of contents, headlines, photos, and key features. As he would go through the weekly edition, he would make mental notes of what he planned to read first, second, and last. About the time he got through the week's edition, it was time to eagerly start the process over the next Thursday.

What Mark didn't realize at the time is that he was using the technique that reading teachers and researchers call previewing and skimming. These types of actions, along with using gaming concepts, are both really effective ways to engage and motivate students. This chapter discusses this pair of strategies.

Preassessment: Skimming

When students in the classroom use *skimming*, they accomplish three things: they (1) activate prior knowledge related to the material in order to enhance comprehension, (2) enhance the speed and accuracy of reading, and (3) clarify the purpose for reading (Young, 2003; Usen, 1993). For these reasons, previewing and skimming content before it is taught can improve comprehension for all learners (Graves, Cooke, & LaBerge, 1983, as cited in Paris et al., 1991; Lynch, 2021).

Often as instructors, after administering an assessment, we would prepare for the next unit by asking students to skim the class textbook to observe key words, headings, photos, graphs, or other key items that will likely be important when the instruction continues. Educational researcher Robert J. Marzano (2016, 2017) includes previewing new material by skimming in his New Art and Science of Teaching framework. When skimming, students "look at major section headings and subheadings and . . . analyze those headings to pick out main ideas and important concepts in the passage" (Marzano, 2017, p. 54). Then they can summarize passages, recording what they think they already know and predicting what they think they will learn (Marzano, 2017). To us, this is a simple and efficient activity that allows all students to engage in a highly effective strategy to engage their future learning and, for some, determine which students already know the material. If, after completing this activity, teachers can see that certain students understand what they are going to teach, they can use a question 4 strategy. Here are the steps we recommend.

1. As an introductory activity for the upcoming unit, provide students with the student skimming handout in figure 6.1. The reproducible version appears on page 101.

Unit: ______________________ Name: ______________________

As you prepare for the upcoming unit, list the key items, words, and phrases you see in the headings, subheadings, illustrations, and bolded items that you anticipate being important during this unit.

Headings	**What do you already know about this topic?**	**What do you think you will learn about this topic during this unit?**	**On a scale of 1–5, what is your personal interest level in this area?**

Illustrations and Graphs	What do you already know about this topic?	What do you think you will learn about this topic during this unit?	On a scale of 1–5, what is your personal interest level in this area?

Bolded Items	What do you already know about this topic?	What do you think you will learn about this topic during this unit?	On a scale of 1–5, what is your personal interest level in this area?

Figure 6.1: Student skimming handout.

2. Collect the completed handouts.
3. Analyze the results of the inventories with the collaborative team. Determine which students could qualify for question 4 support. As with any preassessment, a conversation with the students to confirm their level of understanding will be necessary.

Question 4 Strategy: Gaming

Growing up, we loved playing games of all kinds. Board games like Stratego, Risk, and Life occupied us for hours with our friends and family members. We also loved video games *Pitfall, Tecmo Bowl,* and *Mike Tyson's Punch-Out.* This hasn't changed among the students we have taught. With game applications on smartphones and video games with amazing, life-like graphics, people are playing games even more frequently. In fact, it has been estimated that people around the world spend three billion hours a week playing games (McGonigal, 2010). And games are also finding their way into educational settings. According to one study, 55 percent of K–8 teachers, specifically, use digital games in the classroom at least weekly and 80 percent at least monthly; more than 60 percent of teachers themselves engage in digital gaming at least once a week (Takeuchi & Vaala, 2014).

That's a lot of gaming.

It doesn't appear that the gaming industry and its connection to education are going away any time soon. Digital citizenship expert Carrie Rogers-Whitehead (2021) writes about how the gaming industry can boost education. She discusses the increase in the popularity of esports from a mainstream perspective, the number of not just students but parents who are gamers, and viewership of live streaming services such as Twitch (www.twitch.tv). She uses these reasons to highlight that gaming and Twitch streams are not going away or diminishing and represent a great opportunity to better connect with and educate our students (Rogers-Whitehead, 2021).

Gaming or gamification is something that has gained a lot of traction in education circles. While the research is mixed on whether it is effective (Smiderle, Rigo, Marques, Coelho, & Jaques, 2020), there is little wonder why educators are intrigued. Some see gaming as a creative way to engage students in a way that will interest them; others see it as a distraction. As with any other instructional strategy, gamification's effectiveness depends on the student (Smiderle et al., 2020), but it's undeniably a strong addition to the teacher toolbox. After all, games and gaming engage students with an intense focus, encouraging friends and strangers together to enthusiastically collaborate, coordinate, trust one another, and work toward a common goal. What if we could tap into this focus and motivation with our learners? What if students came to, for example, mathematics class as ready to learn as they are when they get together to play a game with friends?

The question becomes, how do we, as educators, tap into this seemingly innate human urge to play games? And, how do we make sure that the games we create for students inspire deeper thinking and don't end up rewarding minimal effort and repetitive tasks? Entire books, conferences, and journals have been dedicated to this topic. Some examples include books on gamification and gaming in the classroom such as *Explore Like a Pirate: Gamification and Game-Inspired Course Design to Engage, Enrich, and Elevate Your Learners* by Michael Matera (2015), *Gamify Your Classroom: A Field Guide to Game-Based Learning (New Literacies and Digital Epistemologies)* by Matthew Farber (2015), and *Game On!: Gamification, Gameful Design, and the Rise of the Gamer Educator* by Kevin Bell (2018). The University of Michigan Library offers a database (https://bit.ly/3n251cL) of a number of key journals dedicated to computer and video game study and peer-reviewed research. One lesson we have learned from exploring these areas is that there is no one best way to incorporate games into the classroom. The design of the game and its ability to incorporate the content being taught in an engaging way are critically important.

In a podcast made for a regional summit on personalized learning, presenter Michael Matera (Westside Personalized, 2018) breaks down the types of games that teachers can look to in their classrooms into the following components.

- **Gamification:** This is when you take something familiar and make a game from it. In a given course, an instructor would take familiar concepts and ideas and determine strategies, such as badges, leaderboards, and earning points for correct answers. Coffee shops and restaurants offering points per visit to earn free products and fitness centers posting leaderboards for daily performance of members are examples of taking something traditional and adding game play.
- **Game-based learning:** This refers to taking a familiar game and determining what makes it engaging. For example, in the board game Life, participants enjoy making decisions based on what they think will help them live their best lives and then relying on chance to learn about how their lives go. Thinking of these game mechanics, what content from a course could you consider and then place into a game that mimics the mechanics of a familiar game such as Life? Perhaps a class on personal finance becomes a game with statistics on earning potential for possible jobs, costs of college tuition, and other statistics, which become the foundation for the traditional game.
- **Game play:** This refers to something purchased, ready to play right off the shelf. For example, anyone that has played a marathon session of Risk has emerged with a much better understanding of the size and location of various countries. One might argue that a few sessions of playing this game could help a student learn the countries of the world.

With these components in mind, here are the steps we recommend for gaming in the classroom.

1. Visit with the students who demonstrate through the skimming activity that they have a strong understanding of the content. Talk about where they got their information from and ask for more information to learn about their true understanding.
2. Once done with your student conversations, determine which students will receive question 4 strategies. Share with the question 4 students that they will be working on an alternative assignment for the upcoming unit. Also, explain to them that they will have a choice of working alone or in a small group once the assignment is shared.
3. Ask the students to complete the games handout in figure 6.2 (see the reproducible version on page 104).

Complete items 1–4 individually and 5–7 as a team.

1. What games have you played in the last year for fun? (Think of video games, board games, or just a game made up with a friend.)
2. Of these games, which are your favorite?
3. What is it you like about your favorite games? (Be specific.)
4. Thinking of your favorite games and what you have skimmed, what are some ideas you have for making a learning game out of this unit?

Gamification: This is when you take something familiar and make a game from it.

Is there a way to make a game out of this unit? (Think leaderboards, badges, or points for correct answers.)

Game-based learning: Adapt a familiar game by determining what makes it engaging and apply those mechanics to class content.

Is there a game you enjoy playing that could be modified to suit this unit?

Game play: Use an existing game as a way to learn content.

Is there a game you know of that would help you learn material for this unit if you and others played it?

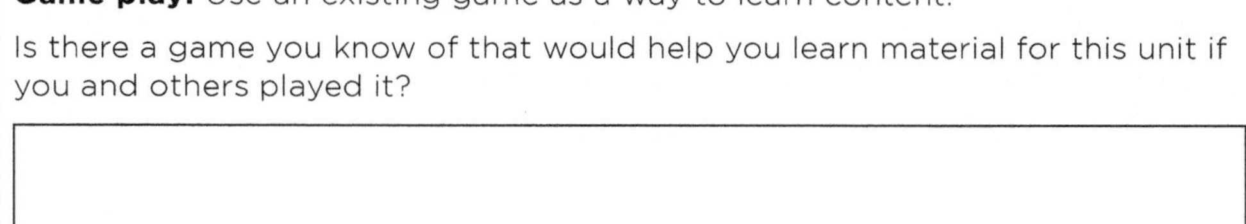

5. Share your responses with your team. As a team, you will develop a game for this unit using elements of gamification, game-based learning, game play, or all three. The game you come up with will be used with the class in one fashion or another.
6. As a team, determine five different ideas and strategies for a game your team could use for this unit.
7. Of these ideas, which were your favorite? What made them your favorite? Do parts of one idea connect to other ideas?
8. Work to develop a consensus on the game that you will develop and share with the class.

Source: Adapted from Matera (Westside Personalized, 2018).

Figure 6.2: Student games handout.

4. By completing the games handout, students will be able to develop their game. If time allows, provide opportunities for classmates to play the game as a review for the unit assessment.

Example 1: Second-Grade Science

A second-grade team is starting its science unit on plants with the essential standards focused on the structure of plants, the purposes of parts of a plant, and photosynthesis. The teacher team provides each student with two nonfiction text passages that focus on these three essential science standards. The students then receive the student skimming handout (figure 6.1, page 93) and around thirty minutes to read the two passages and then fill out the handout. Once the students finish the handout, the three second-grade teachers set aside time at their next collaborative meeting to look at the handouts to determine which students they would consider question 4 students. Based on the student skimming results, they determine that a total of twelve students among the three classrooms qualify for question 4 support for the science unit.

The team groups the twelve students into four teams of three and asks them to complete the student games handout (figure 6.2). The teachers have not previously done skimming and gaming with their students, so they decide to give each question 4 student team a game idea choice bank to provide them with game ideas. Here are the game options.

- Board game
- *Jeopardy!* game
- Kahoot! game
- ChatterPix game

Once the student teams complete the student games handout and choose their game option, one of the teachers spends time with each question 4 student team in order to make sure members are on the right track regarding game development and to provide any needed guidance. The second-grade teachers agree to have the question 4 students in the classroom for some of the whole group's plant and photosynthesis curricular work, but they also carve out time for the teams to meet. During this question 4 student team time, students work together in the hallway pod to create their game and develop their game questions. Teachers task the teams with having their games ready to play in order to support all of the second-grade students on the review day before the summative assessment. Two of the four teams develop simple hands-on board games that use dice and question cards, while the other two teams use their iPad applications to create a Kahoot! and a ChatterPix game that could be used by the whole class on the SmartBoard. The teacher who is supporting the question 4 students checks in with the teams periodically during the unit to ensure that each team is developing a quality game with questions focused on the appropriate standards. The day before the review day, the question 4 students each play each other's games and give feedback to refine or improve the game. On the day before the plant unit summative assessment, the question 4 student teams each have time during class to present their games to the other students, and the students in the classroom have the option to play them as part of their review for the upcoming tests.

Example 2: High School Physical Education

A high school physical education department has just completed a curriculum review process and found that the community wants a focus on the individual health and growth of each student. As a result, four years of physical education have become a requirement for graduation, and an elective called Personalized PE becomes popular. In this course, each student sets an individual fitness or health goal for the year and then works with the teacher and other students to meet the goal. Teachers of this course meet regularly and use data about student progress toward their goals as their data-informed conversations during collaborative team time.

Every day of the class, students receive time during the class period to work on their goals in whatever way they want. This could include stretching, weightlifting, or a cardiovascular-based workout. The one condition is that they must have their heart rate elevated above 120 for at least twenty minutes of class, which is monitored with a heart rate monitor. Early on in the class, they find that a common question emerged from the students: "What should I do for my twenty minutes?"

To answer this question, the teacher team begins preparing a workout of the day (WOD) for the students to use if they want. The workouts are competitive in nature and measure how quickly or how many rounds a student can perform of the exercises they put together. Some of the workouts are individual, some take place with a partner, and others require a larger team. Students who do not need or want to compete in the WOD are allowed to get their heart rate up in any way they want, and they can pursue an activity in a different way. In fact, a team of four plays and giggles while they take part in good old-fashioned tag for twenty minutes on a regular basis.

For students who choose the more challenging workouts, the WOD is listed on the whiteboard, on the class website, and on the accompanying class-specific app. Before the official workout begins during the class period, students are required to individually and quickly read a short article or website and watch videos of the movements they will perform in the WOD. After completing this skimming activity, students are required to send the instructor a short video of them completing one of each of the exercises before beginning. As instructors view the videos, they would make their way to individual students to address any errors before setting a timer. This short activity ensures all students who choose the challenging workout understand what they are to do and use proper form.

To create a little excitement, the teachers begin creating leaderboards for those completing the challenging WOD on a daily basis, which are published on the class website and app. While some students don't want anything to do with the more intense workouts and leaderboards, others thrive on it. Students compete with one another and regularly look at how other students do throughout the day as the board is updated. The teacher regularly talks with the students about practicing integrity and encouraging each other on a daily basis. At the end of the day, a computerized awards ceremony honors the first-, second-, and third-place finishers in different categories for the day by having student-generated avatars receive medals. Students' avatars act as visual depictions that students see when the teacher hands out award for the top finishers in each class, as well as most improved and hardest worker. The energy and excitement that come from this daily occurrence generate buzz for the school and make physical education one of the most popular classes there.

Chapter Reflection

In chapter 9 (page 127), you will review what you have learned and tried from each chapter to make future planning decisions to determine which strategies will work best for your team. To assist in this, consider the following questions.

Preassessment Reflection Questions: Skimming

1. Did this strategy help your team identify question 4 students?
2. Did this strategy take a reasonable amount of teacher time to implement?
3. Did this strategy take a reasonable amount of classroom time to implement?
4. Can you see your team using this strategy for future units to determine which students already know the material?

Question 4 Strategy Reflection Questions: Gaming

1. Were students able to succeed as a result of this strategy?
2. Was this strategy easy for teachers to use?
3. Was this challenging for students?
4. Was this engaging for students?
5. Can you see your team using this strategy for future units to challenge students who already know the material?

Student Skimming Handout

Unit: ____________________ Name: ____________________

As you prepare for the upcoming unit, list the key items, words, and phrases you see in the headings, subheadings, illustrations, and bolded items that you anticipate being important during this unit.

Headings	What do you already know about this topic?	What do you think you will learn about this topic during this unit?	On a scale of 1–5, what is your personal interest level in this area?

Illustrations and Graphs	What do you already know about this topic?	What do you think you will learn about this topic during this unit?	On a scale of 1–5, what is your personal interest level in this area?

Bolded Items	What do you already know about this topic?	What do you think you will learn about this topic during this unit?	On a scale of 1–5, what is your personal interest level in this area?

Student Games Handout

Complete items 1–4 individually and 5–7 as a team.

1. What games have you played in the last year for fun? (Think of video games, board games, or just a game made up with a friend.)

2. Of these games, which are your favorite?

3. What is it you like about your favorite games? (Be specific.)

4. Thinking of your favorite games and what you have skimmed, what are some ideas you have for making a learning game out of this unit?

Gamification: This is when you take something familiar and make a game from it.

Is there a way to make a game out of this unit? (Think leaderboards, badges, or points for correct answers.)

Game-based learning: Adapt a familiar game by determining what makes it engaging and apply those mechanics to class content.

Is there a game you enjoy playing that could be modified to suit this unit?

Game play: Use an existing game as a way to learn content.

Is there a game you know of that would help you learn material for this unit if you and others played it?

page 1 of 2

5. Share your responses with your team. As a team, you will develop a game for this unit using elements of gamification, game-based learning, game play, or all three. The game you come up with will be used by the class in one fashion or another.

6. As a team, determine five different ideas and strategies for a game your team could use for this unit.

7. Of these ideas, which were your favorite? What made them your favorite? Do parts of one idea connect to other ideas?

8. Work to develop a consensus on the game that you will develop and share with the class.

Source: Adapted from Matera (Westside Personalized, 2018).

Reference

Westside Personalized. (2018, June). *A conversation with Michael Matera, author of "Explore like a pirate" (ep. 65)* [Audio podcast]. Accessed at https://podcasts.apple.com/us/podcast/conversation-michael-matera-author-explore-like-pirate/id1328946316?i=1000437633612&l=es on August 12, 2021.

CHAPTER 7

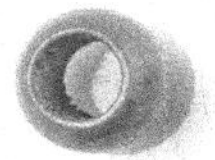  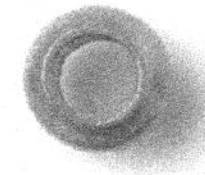 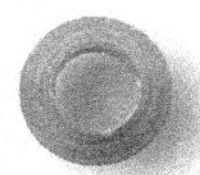 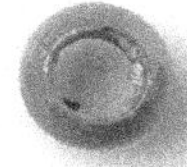 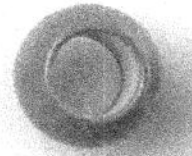 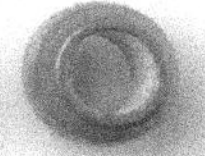

Showing What I Know With Projects and the Hook

Sometimes students will just surprise you with the knowledge and drive they have about a certain subject area. When he was a young elementary student, coauthor Mark, for some reason, enjoyed learning about past presidents. Is it any wonder that he became a social studies teacher? His knowledge of presidents went deeper than memorizing the order of who preceded whom. He enjoyed reading about their lives and the types of experiences they had before becoming president. If he had a choice for a project while in class growing up, he would immediately pick a topic that would cover a president because he knew he would have that interest. Needless to say, projects and assignments are so much more enjoyable if they are on a topic that you want to learn more about.

With projects, students take little, if any, class time to demonstrate what they have learned. Teachers give them the option to go home and develop a project or bring in artifacts to demonstrate what they know. In our experience, students who are interested in a subject area may blow you away with what they bring to you. We have seen students bring in everything from a recreated Civil War battlefield made from art materials to an intricate model with pulleys demonstrating photosynthesis. All of these were completed by students prior to the current unit and course; they represented activities that the students had done in a previous class or on their own. Because you and your team may, over the years, develop quite a collection of usable artifacts that other students will also find interesting, *the hook*—a method of helping students connect with upcoming learning—is a perfect pairing with student-developed projects. This chapter discusses both.

Preassessment: Projects

One way to learn about what students know about a certain subject is to ask students to share what evidence of knowledge they have on a certain topic with you. Students might provide photos, artifacts, collectibles, awards, videos, social media collections, portfolios, or scrapbook items. Sometimes, they might actually research and produce a new project—or bring one they've created in the past. If students are learning about and researching topics on their own time that you are studying in class, this is a great indication that they already know it. A student who has photos of herself accepting awards at a 4H contest for horticulture would likely know something in a middle school class covering botany. A student who has videos of himself presenting at a speech contest might be able to stretch himself with a different assignment for an introductory speech in an English class.

Student projects and artifacts provide a picture of what students already know and are passionate about. If students have a passion and are looking forward to sharing this with you in a project about an upcoming unit, it will feel easy for them, and they will be excited to share. If the content you are about to cover is any area where they have no background or experience, they don't need to worry about a thing. There is really no class time lost for either group of students.

Please note that what we are proposing for our question 4 students is not *problem*-based learning; this is *project*-based learning. Projects take place at home without the teacher's help. Problem-based learning is when the entire class explores real-world problems, develops appropriate questions to address the challenge, and then develops a plan to solve the problem. A project is an activity students do on their own, at home, if they want to share and demonstrate a passion and knowledge they have for a certain subject area (Watanabe-Crockett, 2014).

As with all of the common assessments in this book done prior to the unit lesson, the information teachers gather from student projects is a starting point. Even if students have items related to an upcoming unit, they may not necessarily become question 4 students for that unit. The next step is always to meet with the student to discuss the topic and get an overview of the student's knowledge of this topic. When it is clear that the student understands the material at a high level, the teacher can provide an alternate assignment. Here are the steps we recommend for student projects as preassessment.

1. Develop a summary statement that provides an overall glimpse into what students will be learning in this unit.
2. With a few days of warning, share the student worksheet (figure 7.1). See the reproducible version on page 116.

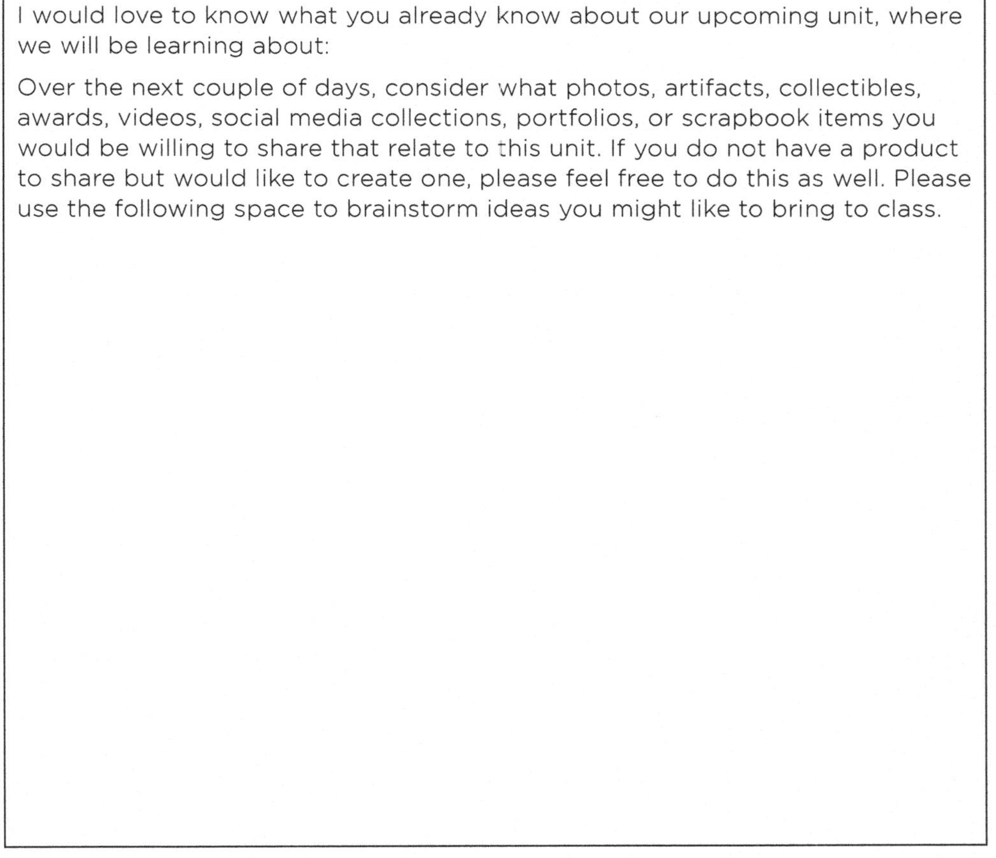
I would love to know what you already know about our upcoming unit, where we will be learning about:

Over the next couple of days, consider what photos, artifacts, collectibles, awards, videos, social media collections, portfolios, or scrapbook items you would be willing to share that relate to this unit. If you do not have a product to share but would like to create one, please feel free to do this as well. Please use the following space to brainstorm ideas you might like to bring to class.

Figure 7.1: Student project handout.

3. Assign students who have proven a deep understanding of the subject area following a conversation the question 4 strategy for this chapter.

Question 4 Strategy: The Hook

We first heard about engaging or hooking all students with an activity when they enter the room the way most educators in our age group did—by learning about Madeline Hunter's (1982) model of mastery learning. In the 1960s, she developed a widely known and accepted model for teachers developing lesson plans, which has since been updated and expanded (Hunter, 2004). Her very first step in this process is to create an anticipatory set, or *hook*, to engage students and create interest in what they are about to learn. Feeling engaged and active right from the start, as opposed to coming into the classroom and sitting down waiting to begin, changes the way the classroom operates (Gonzalez, 2014).

Anticipatory sets can range from handouts to hands-on activities to any other creative idea that connects to the day's or unit's learning. There are a number of resources that exist for creatively engaging students with a hook. One resource shares ideas such as leaving three to four special items on a table near the door each day that students can look forward to seeing, playing a guessing game, sharing a video or podcast, leaving a hint for what is to come, or dressing up as a character or famous person you will be studying (Phillips, 2019). Another writer, Alison Smith (2021), shares hook ideas such as creating a theme for the classroom, creating "feely boxes," conducting surveys and graphs, going on classroom "museum" walks, playing games, posing questions, and using kinesthetic or musical hooks. The commonality these share is that they all engage the students at various points of a unit to obtain their attention and get them excited about what they are going to learn.

Educators and authors Grant Wiggins and Jay McTighe (1998), well known for their work on curriculum design and the importance of having an end in mind in learning, have also expanded on this type of activity. In their work, they describe the acronym WHERETO as a process for ensuring that the learning activities to accompany the curriculum and assessment writing are aligned with a clear purpose. The H in WHERETO requires teachers to think about the hook and hold. What is going to hook and hold students' interest and enthusiasm at the beginning of each lesson? Examples of ways to hook students in their work include using odd facts and examples, provocative questions, challenges, problems, simulations, and technology connections (Wiggins & McTighe, 1998).

The hook takes planning and preparation because you and your team will be developing stations for the students to kick off the lesson. With some of the other ideas in this book, the students take the lead in the work, and the teacher is the mentor in the middle. In the hook, the teacher or collaborative team develops these stations before teaching begins. This is a great way to engage all students in what they will experience in the upcoming unit, and it can serve as a way to challenge and push question 4 students in a way that is the most subtle and least noticeable to the rest of the class. For this unit, we recommend adapting two of what gifted education professor and researcher Colleen Willard-Holt (2003) identifies as the five most significant ways of supporting learners who already know the material: (1) curriculum compacting, (2) flexible grouping, (3) tiered assignments, (4) produce choice, and (5) multilevel learning stations. From these options, we like to use *tiered activities*, which is when students work side by side with other students on the same objective, but at different challenge or difficulty levels. We also recommend *multitiered learning stations*, which are typically learning stations set up at the start of a unit to create interest.

By combining tiered activities with learning stations, an excellent question 4 strategy will also support all of the students in the class. In the hook, teachers set up stations tied to the essential learning outcome for the unit and develop multiple activities representing the range of what they expect of students. One station might have basic activities, activities with a bit more challenge, and activities with an even larger challenge. The most successful stations that we have seen are those that provide numerous choices for each level of challenge.

As a team, you will want to think about the key concepts that you will be teaching over the next three to four weeks, and determine the types of items and activities that will draw in the students. Coauthor Mark worked with one team that was teaching nonfiction writing to second-grade students. To hook students in, one of the teachers asked students to bring in a photo of them doing their favorite activity. Once students entered the room, they were randomly provided one of their classmates' photos and given the assignment to write a fictional story about what they see in the photo. When completed, students shared their fictional story with the owner of the photograph. Then, the teacher instructed the students to share what really happened with their classmate who made up the story about their photograph. The students got to learn more about their classmates and grasped the difference between a fiction and nonfiction story in a fun and entertaining way. In this scenario, students who already knew it in language arts had a wonderful opportunity to shine by showing creativity, writing skills, and storytelling ability. After this introduction, all students were enthused and excited to tell their real story.

In secondary multitier learning stations, stations can be organized by standard or objective. Coauthor Mark writes about a middle school history team in Olentangy, Ohio, in *When They Already Know It* (Weichel et al., 2018) that demonstrates the power of using stations in its work. Team members developed stations at the end of the unit, set up around each key standard, as a way for students to show they were ready to take an assessment. Each station required beginning, proficient, and advanced skills. Students were engaged in their learning and had results that far exceeded student performance from past years when stations were not used. Stations a student might find interesting include video clips, editorials, makeshift museums, and social media postings. Each hook station featured questions or activities at various levels.

The hook is paired with the preassessment strategy of projects because of the potential for you and your team to use the items students bring to demonstrate what they already know. Most students who see their areas of passion demonstrated for the whole class will certainly be engaged and excited to be included as a key contributor to the class.

Here are the steps we recommend for using the hook in the classroom.

1. Brainstorm the type of hooks your team might use in the upcoming unit. Ideas could include the following: playing a game, putting items on display, showing a video, playing a podcast, creating an escape room, role playing, giving a speech, analyzing graphs and charts, conducting a lab or experiment, arranging a museum walk, playing relevant music, conducting a physical activity, or other ideas your team develops.
2. From your brainstormed list for this unit, determine which might work for this class. Consider how best to engage students and create a hook for upcoming learning.
3. Determine the best time to use the hooks you have chosen. Does it make sense to start the unit with this hook, or would it work better at another time in the unit?
4. Begin planning as a team to incorporate the hooks you have agreed on. Be sure to consider how to think and work smarter and not harder as you develop your plan.

Example 1: Third Grade

A third-grade collaborative team meets at the beginning of an interdisciplinary unit that focuses on STEM education and English language arts. The lesson is inspired by training and professional development as part of a schoolwide initiative to focus on inquiry. The team proudly develops a unit around simple machines where students learn about science standards about planning and conducting an investigation, making observations and measurements, asking questions, and defining a simple design problem. The unit's culminating activity occurs when students take bird's-eye-view photos of toys that they bring from home, develop questions about the design, and create a poem using the formula similar to the popular "I Spy" books.

As teachers of third-grade students will tell you, students who walk in the door ready to excel in this type of activity are typically eager to share this with their teacher. A week before the start of the unit, the teacher announces to the class and shares in the weekly parent newsletter email for the classroom that they will soon be beginning a unit on simple machines. Students who have this as an existing hobby and passion are encouraged to see the teacher in the next week.

When students and parents make their way to the teacher to share this interest area, the teacher probes for examples and artifacts that will help demonstrate the skill of building a simple machine. This sharing could be done by looking at past social media posts, videos, pictures, or even better, by bringing in an actual product that a student has previously built. Once shared, the teacher asks questions that demonstrate the student's knowledge of the projects. Probing questions will show the teacher what the student knows about this work.

Students who demonstrate this prior knowledge and interest are assigned to a special group where they will have a choice to take on a special challenge. While students in the rest of the class will be asked to bring in a toy that will be labeled with key terms, which will be photographed and then written about in a poem, this team will be given a chance to learn about Rube Goldberg machines through a series of videos and text passages. Rube Goldberg machines are complex designs that attempt to accomplish a simple task. The internet is full of sample projects and ideas using these principles. Then, students have the opportunity to build their own contraptions, which will be a much greater challenge than the rest of the students in the class.

Once the question 4 students bring in examples they have developed prior to the unit, an additional component to this unit is that the teacher will allow students to study and examine an exemplar project before they begin a similar yet less involved activity. Another additional learning opportunity and hook used for the class is allowing all the extension students an opportunity to be a part of a panel discussion where they have the chance to share their passion and ideas for simple machines. This panel discussion could also be turned into a podcast for parents, and future classes could learn from their work.

Example 2: Seventh-Grade Social Studies

A seventh-grade social studies collaborative team is beginning a unit in which members will lead the students in a series of activities, lessons, and assessments that center around ancient civilizations such as Mesopotamia, Egypt, the Indus Valley, Greece, and Rome. The team discusses how, in years past, some students came to class as experts on one or more of the civilizations because it was of personal interest to them. This year, the team decides to capitalize on this interest and provide a more engaging experience for their students.

As the unit prior to the one about ancient civilizations is wrapping up, the teachers take a few minutes from class to give a quick overview of the unit that will soon start. They inform students that if anyone has a particular interest or passion in one or more of these civilizations, they should bring any evidence from home that would show some work they have done in this area. Teachers emphasize that pictures, anything they have made, videos, or writing would suffice.

Over the course of the next few weeks, various students bring in interesting items from home. One student brings replicas of ancient Egyptian artifacts. Another student brings a comic book he made about the rise and fall of ancient Rome. Yet another student brings a painting she made about ancient Greece and the Olympics. While these are wonderful items, none show evidence of being a question 4 student for this unit. The conversations the teacher has with the students confirm this to be true. However, the students are excited about the idea of the teacher using the items they have brought in at a station for the first day of their upcoming unit on ancient civilizations. The collaborative team sets up stations all around the room, including those using artifacts from the students, that would create interest and buzz around the topic they will be learning about for the next three weeks.

There is one student, however, who shows why question 4 student common assessments such as projects are important to consider. After receiving this assignment, one student spends two weeks putting together an animated video outlining the key concepts covered in the textbook regarding the Roman Empire. The animations, movements, and text are spot on and even include a dramatization of Julius Caesar's assassination with accompanying scary music. After a short conversation with this student, it is clear that he probably doesn't need to do the same activities with the rest of the class when they spend time on Rome. For that part of the lesson, the teacher and student could work out a mini-contract for a short activity to work on a different and deeper assignment. In the meantime, the video provides a perfect segue into the unit—one that the teacher can use for years to come.

Chapter Reflection

In chapter 9 (page 127), you will review what you have learned and tried from each chapter to make future planning decisions to determine which strategies will work best for your team. To assist in this, consider the following questions.

Preassessment Reflection Questions: Projects

1. Did this strategy help your team identify question 4 students?
2. Did this strategy take a reasonable amount of teacher time to implement?
3. Did this strategy take a reasonable amount of classroom time to implement?
4. Can you see your team using this strategy for future units to determine which students already know the material?

Question 4 Strategy Reflection Questions: The Hook

1. Were students able to succeed as a result of this strategy?
2. Was this strategy easy for teachers to use?
3. Was this challenging for students?
4. Was this engaging for students?
5. Can you see your team using this strategy for future units to challenge students who already know the material?

Student Project Handout

I would love to know what you already know about our upcoming unit, where we will be learning about: ____________________

Over the next couple of days, consider what photos, artifacts, collectibles, awards, videos, social media collections, portfolios, or scrapbook items you would be willing to share that relate to this unit. If you do not have a product to share but would like to create one, please feel free to do this as well. Please use the following space to brainstorm ideas you might like to bring to class.

CHAPTER 8

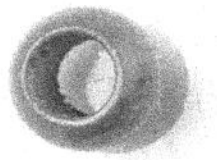 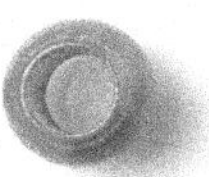 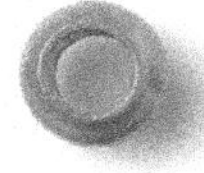 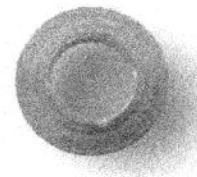 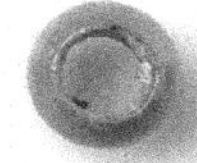 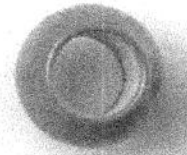 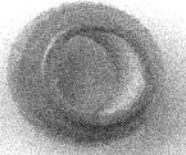

Showing What I Know With Unit Tests and Problem-Solving Teams

If you have been following along in this book by trying a new preassessment strategy paired with a question 4 strategy each month, chances are that you are getting pretty good at this! You have gotten into a familiar rhythm where you look over the key pieces of what you are going to be teaching, quickly analyze what students know with one of the strategies, and then provide personalized instructional activities where students work alone or on a team to demonstrate their learning in a different way.

In chapter 2 (page 33), we ask you and your collaborative teams to consider developing a short multiple-choice test to provide students to determine who already has a grasp of the material being presented. In this chapter, we ask you to take this idea one step further, and quite frankly, this could be less work for you and your team members. We are suggesting that you ask your students to try taking the final unit exam before teaching the unit.

Please note that we are not suggesting that you give the exact test, enabling students to memorize the order of the questions and the order in which the answer choices appear. We wouldn't want students trying to remember that number 1 is b, number 2 is d, and so on. We are suggesting that by sharing the content of the exam, you are benefiting the students who already know the material and the rest of the students in the class by giving them a clear and specific idea of what you expect them to know at the end of the unit.

Many of you might be asking, "Isn't this cheating? Isn't this just teaching to the test?" We would contend that it isn't cheating, and it *is* teaching to the test. To be clear, we're saying that teaching to the test is not a bad thing. In one of our favorite presentations on best practices in grading, our hero, author and professor Thomas Guskey (2010), shoots down the myth that we shouldn't teach to the test. Providing the questions from the test is different from giving someone the answers. Doing so simply means that you're being clear and concise with the learner about what the learner should study. Guskey (2010) provides real-life examples, such as new drivers taking a driver's exam or would-be pilots testing for a pilot's license, where providing the questions ahead of time is common and accepted. You know what is on the test, and now your job is to go and learn the material. This chapter discusses using unit tests as preassessments, as well as how this practice can tie in with the problem-solving team's strategy.

Preassessment: Unit Tests

Having clarity around the final summative assessment tool could be incredibly valuable for a student. Who wouldn't have wanted that as a student? By being able to view the exam ahead of time, you would have known where to focus your study time, areas that need the most and least attention, and a preview of what is to come in the unit. All these things are beneficial for student learning.

This idea appears in a *New York Times Magazine* article by science reporter Benedict Carey (2014). In it, he examines the impact of taking a test before the material is taught. While you would likely not do well, the author describes other benefits of what is called the *pre-test effect*. He contends that by reviewing the material on the test, students are able to think about and store the information for what will be coming later. The test basically becomes an introduction to what students should learn throughout the unit. It kind of greases the wheels for learning. Further, he argues that offering the unit exam as a preassessment helps all students read questions more carefully, know what to focus on in the notes when studying at a later date, and recognize what to listen for when the teacher mentions specific information (Carey, 2014).

Providing a view of the final unit exam could benefit all students for all these reasons. The natural assumption for students taking a test on an upcoming unit would be a relatively poor performance, as they haven't had this instruction yet. However, what happens when students do perform well before you have provided the instruction? It would imply that these students will sit through several days or maybe even a few weeks of instruction before receiving an exam on which they would perform admirably. This is a perfect opportunity for you, as the instructor, to personalize instruction for these students. Here are the steps we recommend.

1. As a collaborative team, determine what assessment you will use at the end of your upcoming unit. If it is the exact test, take time to rearrange the answer choices, question order, and other components that might be easy for a student to memorize to ensure students don't just memorize a pattern. You want them to learn the content. You want students to be familiar with the content of the final test but not have access to shortcuts.
2. Administer the final unit assessment at the start of the upcoming unit. Be sure no copies leave the room if it is not completed electronically.
3. As a team, grade the test and look for students who demonstrate an understanding of the material. Meet with those students one on one to talk more about how they know this material and where they have learned it beforehand. During this conversation, you will seek to understand areas where you will want to compact the curriculum for the students for this unit.
4. Review the test with the entire class as a way to preview the upcoming unit. Share key ideas that many students already know, areas that they can look forward to learning more about, and things to keep in mind as they study this particular unit.

Question 4 Strategy: Problem-Solving Teams

As we explain at the start of the chapter, providing the final assessment to students in advance of the unit can be a useful, viable preassessment strategy. What can make it so powerful is what you can do with the students after the assessment. We are essentially advocating using the summative assessment in a formative way at the start of the unit. We believe that using the results from your final test will allow you to group students into problem-solving teams when necessary. For instance, if several students have not mastered a concept, the teacher can group them together and guide them through the concept in a more intensive manner. Meanwhile, if you have students who demonstrate proficiency on the final assessment, you can group them together in order to solve a deeper or more complex problem that is connected to the unit content. Finally, if you have a group of students that scores perfectly or close to perfect on the final assessment, you would consider them this unit's question 4 students and place them on their own problem-solving team.

The problem-solving team concept comes from the structure of team-based learning. Part of the theoretical framework related to team-based learning focuses on two things: (1) the teacher as the guide to facilitate learning and (2) using relevant problems with group interaction to promote learning (Hrynchak & Batty, 2012). We believe that these two components are the backbone of what we are advocating with problem-solving teams. Science educator Cynthia Brame (2013) shares, "The teacher establishes the learning objectives and chooses the problems on which the students will focus but then acts as a guide while teams work toward their solution to the problem" (p. 2). Like all the strategies in this book, the problems that the team will work to solve must be connected to the learning objectives of the unit. Additionally, depending on the students and the ideas they have, the teacher can present them with problem ideas, or the students can come up with their own to solve. While the approach we are advocating doesn't include all the components of the team-based learning framework, the research base on this strategy supports higher learning gains and an increase in positive attitudes toward collaboration (Brame, 2013). We believe that the benefits of providing this strategy to your question 4 students make it well worth it to try these steps.

1. As a team, fill out the learning objective sections of the problem-solving team's student handout (figure 8.1, with the reproducible version on page 125). Additionally, the team can choose to fill out the column for potential problems to solve with some examples. We highly recommend that the earlier the grade level, the more the team provides potential or example problems to solve.

Learning Objective	Interest Level (Rate 1–5, with 1 being low and 5 being high)	Potential Problems to Solve

Figure 8.1: Problem-solving teams student handout.

2. Provide the problem-solving teams student handout to all the question 4 students. Their job is to fill out the interest level (1 being low level of interest and 5 being high level of interest) for each learning objective.

3. Collect the student handout and organize the problem-solving teams based on the levels of interest that students share on the form. We recommend teams of three or four students.
4. Have each team meet with one of the grade-level or content-area teachers to brainstorm and determine what problem they will solve related to the learning objective. This conversation will also allow the teacher to potentially push the team toward a particular learning objective or problem to solve that makes sense for the team based on its summative assessment results.
5. Teams will be required to submit the problem-solving team planning form (figure 8.2, with the reproducible version on page 126) to their teacher in order to establish the following.
   - The problem to be solved
   - What the final product will be or look like
   - The time line for teacher check-ins and final submission

Problem to Solve	Final Product	Time Line

Figure 8.2: Problem-solving team planning form.

6. The problem-solving teams and the teacher work together and follow the agreed-on products and time lines established.

Example 1: First Grade

A first-grade collaborative team prepares for an upcoming unit on counting and adding, specifically on standards that call for students to learn numerical relationships and operations. A major focus in curriculum development and professional learning throughout the school has centered around the idea of "math talks" and intentionally engaging students in conversations and inquiry about solving problems. For this unit, the team develops an entire learning plan that unpacks the district curriculum map in a way that will make sense to the team over the next two weeks. On the learning plan, the team marks when key instructional activities, checks for understanding, formative assessments, interventions, and unit tests will take place. With a clear plan for what they want the unit to look like, team members can spend extra time considering how to determine which students already know how to count and add and what to do for them when they demonstrate this knowledge.

Teachers then greet their classes and share that they will begin their unit on counting and adding. Since the unit test asks students to demonstrate these basic skills, the teachers feel like they can get a reasonably good idea of how a student would perform on the unit test by observing how they work on basic counting with various objects. While in other grades it might make sense to provide the actual unit test, to this first-grade team, it seems like a better idea to watch how students use their mathematics skills to assess them in a less formal way.

For the activity, the teachers start by having the students get into small groups. During the mathematics block, they drop hundreds of fake leaves that they purchased at a local hobby store. Then they ask students some basic questions, working their way up to questions that will appear on the actual test in a few weeks. Students use the leaves as tools to demonstrate their skills. Teachers physically make their way around the teams and watch how the students answered and responded. In a short amount of time, it is clear which students walked into the classroom that day already prepared to do well on the final unit test. These students become their own small team on subsequent days during the unit.

Each day, the extension group works with various manipulatives like the leaves and receives different problems to solve than the rest of the class. While the rest of the class is adding and subtracting, this problem-solving team gets problems that will demonstrate their ability to use the distributive property. Questions to stretch students' thinking include items such as, "How would you create sets to form 48 leaves?" By taking the concepts aligned to counting and adding and stretching it to include basic multiplication, students are challenged to think in a new and different way.

Example 2: High School Business

A high school business department team meets to determine department SMART goals for the year. Because many of their courses are taught by one person, they have found that creating a SMART goal can be a significant challenge. The team works together to determine goals and themes they will have for students that represent what they want all students to know and be able to do after taking any business class. One of the themes they settle on is supporting students in having an entrepreneurial spirit. Because of this, every business class develops one unit aligned to this goal from the lens of that particular class. And they mutually agree to make this the first unit of the year so they can build on the idea all year.

They find that students have varying levels of understanding on entrepreneurship, and they want to challenge students who already know the material and those who excel. Through their collaborative team time, team members develop an extension activity that they could use in all business classes during the first unit and throughout the year. The best part of the team's plan is that its upfront work will provide an engaging extension for the entire time students are in their class.

Over the summer, the teachers coordinate with district staff to get a list of businesses that have recently requested to work with schools or have in the past. From there, they met with various representatives about a challenge idea. The entrepreneurial challenge starts by asking businesses for problems they would like help solving. By talking with various companies, the teachers gather a long list of ideas. Next, many of the businesses, when asked, share that they are willing to even contribute funds for student prizes and act as a panel of judges to determine who comes up with the best solutions to the problems.

The team members are excited to share their new lessons with the class when the entrepreneurship units start. Students first receive a unit test to see which concepts they already know. Students who received an A on the unit test get the list of challenges from the businesses listed in descending order from most challenging and time consuming to least. All students get an opportunity to work on the challenge or challenges in this unit; however, the question 4 students are allowed to begin early and take on the more challenging ones by working individually or as teams on the challenge. If a team wins the contest, members divide up the prize money among themselves.

One of the most exciting parts of this challenge to students is that actual prize money is listed with each challenge for first, second, and third place. While the highest number is not over $50, student attention is at an all-time high. Because all business classes are completing their entrepreneurship unit at the same time, all students are competing with each other. The interesting thing about these teams is that they are solving real problems for real businesses with real money on the line with judges from outside of the school.

The other benefit of this activity for the entire business department is that they now have extension activities for the entire year. Every six weeks, the teachers open schoolwide competitions with challenges from local business with the small monetary awards. When students in subsequent units test out early, they can form problem-solving teams and work on their challenges together. At the end of each six-week period, there is a short but fun award ceremony with the business partners handing out checks. Not surprisingly, enrollment in business classes begins to expand, and students at all levels are challenged.

When one of the students shares what is taking place in her business class with her mother, who is an elementary teacher, this idea expands to the elementary level. The business department meets with representatives from the elementary school, and they brainstorm how this challenge activity with rewards could work in any subject area. Instead of actual cash prizes, they talk about how younger students can be equally motivated with school trinkets like pencils and other items like donated food and gift certificates.

Chapter Reflection

In chapter 9 (page 127), you will review what you have learned and tried from each chapter to make future planning decisions to determine which strategies will work best for your team. To assist in this, consider the following questions.

Preassessment Reflection Questions: Unit Tests

1. Did this strategy help your team identify question 4 students?
2. Did this strategy take a reasonable amount of teacher time to implement?
3. Did this strategy take a reasonable amount of classroom time to implement?
4. Can you see your team using this strategy for future units to determine which students already know the material?

Question 4 Strategy Reflection Questions: Problem-Solving Teams

1. Were students able to succeed as a result of this strategy?
2. Was this strategy easy for teachers to use?
3. Was this challenging for students?
4. Was this engaging for students?
5. Can you see your team using this strategy for future units to challenge students who already know the material?

Problem-Solving Teams Student Handout

Learning Objective	Interest Level (Rate 1–5, with 1 being low and 5 being high)	Potential Problems to Solve

Problem-Solving Team Planning Form

Problem to Solve	Final Product	Time Line

CHAPTER 9

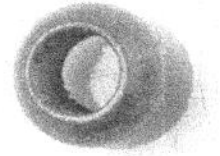 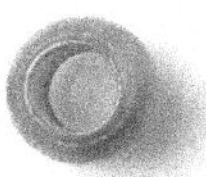 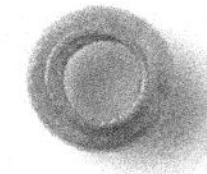  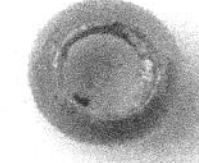 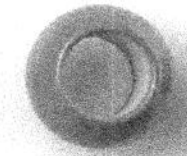 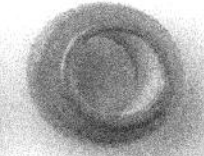

Pulling It All Together

Congratulations! You have done it! Whether you followed along with each unit or tried a few of the common assessments and accompanying question 4 strategies, it is likely that you now have some experience with implementing these strategies. This is good news; most teams we work with across the country self-report that intentional and deliberate planning around question 4 rarely, if ever, happens. By trying these templates with units with which you have familiarity, you are beginning to overcome the most common reasons for not addressing critical question 4.

Now you know how to address question 4. You have ideas and strategies for learning who already knows the material and what they know. Best of all, you have a toolbox of strategies for working with students who already know it. We would argue that these ideas aren't difficult or complicated; any team can address question 4 on a regular basis with the right tools, resources, and desire. It's just a matter of finding the right tools and using them at the right time, which you have hopefully been able to do as a result of this book. Next, we want you to continue thinking about how you will use these ideas to make the most impact for your collaborative team moving forward.

The common formative preassessments and question 4 strategies we grouped together may have worked out perfectly and represent how you want to move forward. However, more than likely, your team had conversations about which strategies worked better than others and how you might have paired the common assessments and question 4 strategies differently. You also might have found that you would use a few of these ideas on a frequent basis and that you might never want to use others. Either of these scenarios is just fine; it is what works best for you and your team that is important. We see the same thing over and over from teams all over the country. For example, one elementary team focusing on mathematics told us that multiple-choice questions and inventories before curriculum compacting would challenge their students. One middle school social studies team determined curriculum compacting and problem-solving teams were the two strategies that they would use with each unit of instruction after giving students part of the unit test to determine who knew the material. A high school English language arts team decided to use KWL charts with badges and problem-solving teams for its question 4 strategies. All of these teams were correct in their decision making because they determined what was right for them. Our goal for each team reading this book is to find your preferred methods and then use them consistently with each unit.

What will work best for your team? What do you think about question 4 strategies moving forward? Looking back on the experiences you had with the last eight chapters, we have a series of reflections your team should consider to further support your team. Please complete the tools on the following pages.

For each question 4 strategy, we shared a sample common assessment. If you were planning a yearlong plan with your collaborative team, what common assessment strategies do you think would work best with which question 4 strategy? Please note, you may pick the same common assessment more than once. In fact, you may determine that there are one or two that become your predictable go-tos for each unit. The correct one to use is the one that your team thinks is the best for your students. (See figure 9.1 and the reproducible version on page 135.)

Of the question 4 strategies we share in this book, which worked the best, which were relatively easy for your team to implement, and which were challenging and engaging for students? These represent the key considerations your team will want to use when determining which strategies will become your go-to selections when your collaborative team moves forward. In figure 9.2 (page 130), we ask that you rank each column with a score of 1, 2, or 3. With this ranking, you are determining if it is not good (1), somewhat good (2), or outstanding (3). Please don't use time assigning scores such as 1.5 and 2.2; assign a 1, 2, or a 3. At the end, review the overall scores you assigned to each strategy. Then, using figure 9.3 (page 131), you can rank the strategies from 1 to 8. This may provide your team with insight as to what strategies you want to focus on moving forward. Reproducible versions of both tools are available on pages 136 and 137.

Thinking of your preferred question 4 strategies and the common assessments that you see best linking to these, now it is time for your team to consider how you will use them for the units that you teach. (See figure 9.4 on page 132 and the reproducible version on page 138.)

Which common assessment strategies do you think would work best with which question 4 strategy?

<table>
<tr><th>Question 4 Strategy</th><th>Your Team's Preferred Common Assessment or Assessments to Use Prior to Unit</th><th>Common Assessment Choices</th></tr>
<tr><td>Curriculum compacting</td><td></td><td rowspan="8">Inventories
Multiple-choice quizzes
KWL charts
Student questions
Drawing
Skimming
Projects
Unit tests</td></tr>
<tr><td>Choice boards</td><td></td></tr>
<tr><td>Alternative assignments</td><td></td></tr>
<tr><td>Question formulation</td><td></td></tr>
<tr><td>Badges</td><td></td></tr>
<tr><td>Gaming</td><td></td></tr>
<tr><td>The hook</td><td></td></tr>
<tr><td>Problem-solving teams</td><td></td></tr>
</table>

Figure 9.1: Question 4 and common assessment best fit.

- In column A of figure 9.4, consider the units that you teach on a regular basis during a school year. In our experience, most educators divide their courses up in three- to four-week units throughout the year. With this thinking in a thirty-six-week school year, you would likely have between nine and twelve units. For elementary school, choose one content area such as mathematics or language arts. For secondary school, think of the course that you spend the most time on.
- In column B, for each unit, determine which of the question 4 strategies your team thinks would be the best fit in that unit.
- In column C, for each unit and considering the question 4 strategy you determined to be the best fit, which common assessment does your team think would work best?

Question 4 feedback: Which strategies worked the best? (1 = not good, 2 = somewhat good, and 3 = outstanding)

Question 4 Strategies	Was this successful? (1, 2, 3)	Was it easy to use? (1, 2, 3)	Was it challenging for students? (1, 2, 3)	Was it engaging for students? (1, 2, 3)	Overall Score
Curriculum compacting					
Choice boards					
Alternative assignments					
Question formulation					
Badges					
Gaming					
The hook					
Problem-solving teams					

Figure 9.2: Question 4 feedback ranking.

Question 4 Strategies	Rank Based on Overall Score
Curriculum compacting	
Choice boards	
Alternative assignments	
Question formulation	
Badges	
Gaming	
The hook	
Problem-solving teams	

Figure 9.3: Question 4 overall ranking.

The next step is for your team to revisit figure 9.4 with each of the units that your team begins. You have done the heavy lifting by thinking about why question 4 is important to consider, trying different strategies, determining which ones work best for your team and curriculum, and analyzing what strategies would work best in each unit.

We encourage and challenge your team to make question 4 a part of your collaborative team process moving forward. Even with the best intentions, it is easy to succumb to the business of the school year and leave good ideas behind. Developing strategies and intentional actions at the start of the year will ensure that they continue, even in months like the one that many educators joke about as being their least favorite of the school year: February. To many, especially those who live in colder areas of the world, this marks a time of year far removed from holiday breaks when the weather is unpleasant, and spring feels like a long time away. We have even heard this month called "angry adult season." But with some planning, teams can ensure things will be seamless even during the most challenging times of year. Teams do many things to make sure that this takes place, including the following.

- Make a team norm to prioritize time for question 4.
- Reserve a set amount of time for question 4 at each collaborative meeting.
- Commit to each other that every unit begins with a common assessment and a plan for those who already know it.

Column A: Units of Study for the Year	Column B: Best Fit Question 4 Strategy	Column C: Best Fit Common Assessment Strategy

Figure 9.4: Question 4 yearly unit plan.

- Perform a self-check on the team's progress once per quarter (see figure 9.5 and the reproducible version on page 139).

QUESTION 4 SCORE SHEET

1 = not at all, 2 = somewhat, and 3 = expert

Our Team: ____________________	Score (circle one)	Steps to Improve
1. Understands who question 4 students are	1 2 3	
2. Understands why we need to address question 4 students	1 2 3	
3. Has made question 4 a part of our team's norms	1 2 3	
4. Has an agreed-on learning plan for each unit	1 2 3	
5. Understands various common assessment choices	1 2 3	
6. Knows which common assessment choices will be used with each unit	1 2 3	
7. Agrees to provide voice, choice, and personalization with question 4 students	1 2 3	
8. Has identified at least three or more question 4 strategies that we can use on a regular basis	1 2 3	
9. Has identified the question 4 strategies that will work best with each of our units	1 2 3	
10. Has made question 4 a regular part of our collaborative team's work	1 2 3	

Figure 9.5: Question 4 score sheet.

We have no doubt that your team is ready and that your students will benefit from your work on question 4. Your collaborative team will soon complete the full, cyclical, ongoing process of addressing all four critical questions of a Professional Learning Community at Work, without omitting the all-important question 4. You will have:

- A system in place where collaborative teams honor their collective commitments and team norms to regularly consider question 4 students
- An easy-to-use toolbox from which, for every unit, you and your team can collaboratively choose a preassessment and matching strategy that will work just right for the question 4 students in your class

- A team that has set the bar for teams schoolwide or districtwide to really address the needs of all learners, including question 4 students

We encourage you to learn from the stories that you and your team members share with each other. Collaboration is at the heart of the PLC at Work process; now it's time to go forth and answer all four critical questions.

Question 4 and Common Assessment Best Fit

Which common assessment strategies do you think would work best with which question 4 strategy?

Question 4 Strategy	Your Team's Preferred Common Assessment or Assessments to Use Prior to Unit	Common Assessment Choices
Curriculum compacting		Inventories Multiple-choice quizzes KWL charts Student questions Drawing Skimming Projects Unit tests
Choice boards		
Alternative assignments		
Question formulation		
Badges		
Gaming		
The hook		
Problem-solving teams		

Question 4 Feedback Ranking

Question 4 feedback: Which strategies worked the best? (1 = not good, 2 = somewhat good, and 3 = outstanding)

Question 4 Strategies	Was this successful? (1, 2, 3)	Was it easy to use? (1, 2, 3)	Was it challenging for students? (1, 2, 3)	Was it engaging for students? (1, 2, 3)	Overall Score
Curriculum compacting					
Choice boards					
Alternative assignments					
Question formulation					
Badges					
Gaming					
The hook					
Problem-solving teams					

Question 4 Overall Ranking

Question 4 Strategies	Rank Based on Overall Score
Curriculum compacting	
Choice boards	
Alternative assignments	
Question formulation	
Badges	
Gaming	
The hook	
Problem-solving teams	

Question 4 Yearly Unit Plan

Column A: Units of Study for the Year	Column B: Best Fit Question 4 Strategy	Column C: Best Fit Common Assessment Strategy

Question 4 Score Sheet

1 = not at all, 2 = somewhat, and 3 = expert

Our Team: ____________	Score (circle one)	Steps to Improve
1. Understands who question 4 students are	1 2 3	
2. Understands why we need to address question 4 students	1 2 3	
3. Has made question 4 a part of our team's norms	1 2 3	
4. Has an agreed-on learning plan for each unit	1 2 3	
5. Understands various common assessment choices	1 2 3	
6. Knows which common assessment choices will be used with each unit	1 2 3	
7. Agrees to provide voice, choice, and personalization with question 4 students	1 2 3	
8. Has identified at least three or more question 4 strategies that we can use on a regular basis	1 2 3	
9. Has identified the question 4 strategies that will work best with each of our units	1 2 3	
10. Has made question 4 a regular part of our collaborative team's work	1 2 3	

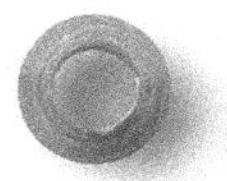

REFERENCES AND RESOURCES

Academic Success Center. (2019, June 4). *Reading strategies: The KWL method.* Accessed at https://asc.tamu.edu/Study-Learning-Handouts-(1)/Reading-Strategies-KWL-Method on December 21, 2021

Anderson, L. W., & Krathwohl, D. R. (Eds.). (2001). *A taxonomy for learning, teaching, and assessing: A revision of Bloom's Taxonomy of educational objectives* (Complete ed.). New York: Longman.

Armstrong, P. (2010). *Bloom's taxonomy.* Accessed at https://cft.vanderbilt.edu/guides-sub-pages/blooms-taxonomy on August 11, 2021.

Bakken, J. P., Obiakor, F. E., & Rotatori, A. F. (Eds.). (2014). *Gifted education: Current perspectives and issues.* Bingley, United Kingdom: Emerald.

Barton, C., & Bennett, T. (2019). *The researchED guide to education myths: An evidence-informed guide for teachers.* Melton, Woodbridge, United Kingdom: John Catt Educational.

Bell, K. (2018). *Game on!: Gamification, gameful design, and the rise of the gamer educator.* Baltimore: Johns Hopkins University Press.

Blended Learning Resources. (n.d.). *Developing multiple choice questions that test higher order thinking.* Accessed at http://blendedlearningresources.co.za/landing-developing-multiple-choice-questions-that-test-higher-order-thinking on August 12, 2021.

Bloom, B. (Ed.). (1954). *Taxonomy of educational objectives: Book 1—The cognitive domain.* New York: Longman.

Boaler, J. (n.d.). *The mathematics of hope: Moving from performance to learning in mathematics classrooms.* Accessed at https://blog.heinemann.com/the-mathematics-of-hope-moving-from-performance-to-learning-in-mathematics-classrooms on September 16, 2021.

Bothell, T. (2018, September 26). *Handouts: 14 rules for writing multiple-choice questions.* Accessed at https://pdf4pro.com/view/handouts-14-rules-for-writing-multiple-choice-questions-5a304e.html on August 11, 2021.

Brame, C. J. (2013). *Team-based learning.* Accessed at https://cft.vanderbilt.edu/guides-sub-pages/team-based-learning on August 11, 2021.

Bray, B., & McClaskey, K. (2015). *Make learning personal: The what, who, WOW, where, and why.* Thousand Oaks, CA: Corwin Press.

Broward County Public Schools. (n.d.) *How to use curriculum compacting to provide personalized enrichment for gifted students.* Accessed at https://browardschools.instructure.com/courses/873274/pages/how-to-use-curriculum-compacting-to-provide-personalized-enrichment-for-gifted-students on December 20, 2021.

Carey, B. (2014, November 22). *Studying for the test by taking it.* Accessed at www.nytimes.com/2014/11/23/sunday-review/studying-for-the-test-by-taking-it.html on September 23, 2021.

de Brey, C., Musu, L., McFarland, J., Wilkinson-Flicker, S., Diliberti, M., Zhang, A., et al. (2019, February). *Status and trends in the education of racial and ethnic groups 2018.* Accessed at https://nces.ed.gov/pubs2019/2019038.pdf on January 4, 2022.

Dickinson, M. (2011). *Writing multiple-choice questions for higher-level thinking.* Accessed at https://learningsolutionsmag.com/articles/804/writing-multiple-choice-questions-for-higher-level-thinking on August 11, 2021.

Diemand-Yauman, C., Oppenheimer, D., & Vaughan, E. (2010, October). Fortune favors the bold (and the italicized): Effects of disfluency on educational outcomes. *Cognition, 118*(1), 111–115.

Dreilinger, D. (2020, October 14). *America's gifted education programs have a race problem. Can it be fixed?* Accessed at www.nbcnews.com/news/education/america-s-gifted-education-programs-have-race-problem-can-it-n1243143 on January 4, 2022.

DuFour, R., DuFour, R., Eaker, R., Many, T. W., & Mattos, M. (2016). *Learning by doing: A handbook for Professional Learning Communities at Work.* Bloomington, IN: Solution Tree Press.

Dweck, C. S. (2015, January 1). *The secret to raising smart kids.* Accessed at www.scientificamerican.com/article/the-secret-to-raising-smart-kids1 on January 7, 2022.

Easton, A. (n.d.). *Westside personalized iCreate.* Accessed at https://sites.google.com/westside66.net/tech-to-help-learners-create/icreate on August 11, 2021.

Farber, M. (2015). *Gamify your classroom: A field guide to game-based learning.* New York: Peter Lang.

Fernandes, M. A., Wammes, J. D., & Meade, M. E. (2018). The surprisingly powerful influence of drawing on memory. *Current Directions in Psychological Science, 27*(5), 302–308. Accessed at https://hsredesign.org/wp-content/uploads/2019/04/Impact-of-drawing-on-memory.pdf on January 5, 2022.

Fisher, R., & Ury, B. (1981). *Getting to yes: Negotiating agreement without giving in* (1st ed.). New York: Penguin.

Gonzalez, J. (2014, September 6). *Know your terms: Anticipatory set.* Accessed at www.cultofpedagogy.com/anticipatory-set on August 11, 2021.

Graves, M. F., Cooke, C. L., & LaBerge, M. J. (1983). Effects of previewing difficult short stories on low ability junior high school students' comprehension, recall, and attitudes. *Reading Research Quarterly, 18*(3), 262–276.

Guskey, T. (2010, October). *Honest and accurate grading policies and practices* [Keynote address]. Ahead of the Curve Assessment Institute, Atlanta, GA.

Hattie, J. A. (2008). *Visible learning: A synthesis of over 800 meta-analyses relating to achievement.* London: Routledge.

Hattie, J. A., Fisher, D., Frey, N., Gojak, L. M., Moore, S. D., & Mellman, W. (2017). *Visible learning for mathematics, grades K–12: What works best to optimize student learning.* Thousand Oaks, CA: Corwin Press.

Hess, K. K., Jones, B. S., Carlock, D., & Walkup, J. R. (2009). *Cognitive rigor: Blending the strengths of Bloom's taxonomy and Webb's Depth of Knowledge to enhance classroom-level processes.* Accessed at https://files.eric.ed.gov/fulltext/ED517804.pdf on September 23, 2021.

Hrynchak, P., & Batty, H. (2012) The educational theory basis of team-based learning. *Medical Teacher, 34*(10), 796–801.

Hunter, M. (1982). *Mastery teaching: Increasing instructional effectiveness in elementary, secondary schools, colleges and universities* (1st ed.). New York: TIP.

Hunter, R. (2004). *Madeline Hunter's mastery teaching: Increasing instructional effectiveness in elementary and secondary schools* (Revised ed.). Thousand Oaks, CA: Corwin Press.

Juliani, A. J. (2020, December). *The ultimate guide to choice boards and learning menus.* Accessed at http://ajjuliani.com/the-ultimate-guide-to-choice-boards-and-learning-menus on August 11, 2021.

Kaufman, S. B. (2019, May 9). *Rethinking gifted education with Scott Peters* (no. 164) [Podcast]. Accessed at https://scottbarrykaufman.com/podcast/rethinking-gifted-education-with-scott-peters on January 7, 2022.

Kelly, B. R. (2019, April 2). *Racial bias associated with disparities in disciplinary action across U.S. schools.* Accessed at www.princeton.edu/news/2019/04/02/racial-bias-associated-disparities-disciplinary-action-across-us-schools on January 4, 2022.

Knight, J. (2013). *High-impact instruction: A framework for great teaching.* Thousand Oaks, CA: Corwin Press.

Kramer, S., & Schul, S. (2017). *School improvement for all: A how-to guide for doing the right work.* Bloomington, IN: Solution Tree Press.

Lockhart, K., Meyer, M. S., & Crutchfield, K. (2022, February). A content analysis of selected state plans for gifted and talented education. *Journal of Advanced Academics, 33*(1), 3–42.

Lynch, M. (2021, March 12). *Skimming: A reading comprehension tool.* Accessed at www.theedadvocate.org/skimming-a-reading-comprehension-tool on December 21, 2021.

Marzano, R. J. (2006). *Classroom assessment and grading that work.* Alexandria, VA: Association for Supervision and Curriculum Development.

Marzano, R. J. (2016). *The Marzano compendium of instructional strategies.* Bloomington, IN: Marzano Resources.

Marzano, R. J. (2017). *The new art and science of teaching.* Bloomington, IN: Solution Tree Press.

Marzano, R. J., Pickering, D. J., & Pollock, J. E. (2001). *Classroom instruction that works: Research-based strategies for increasing student achievement.* Alexandria, VA: Association for Supervision and Curriculum Development.

Matera, M. (2015). *Explore like a pirate: Gamification and game-inspired course design to engage, enrich, and elevate your learners.* San Diego, CA: Dave Burgess Consulting.

May, C. (2014, February 3). *The origin of marketing Vegas: What happens in Vegas stays in Vegas.* Accessed at www.illumine8.com/the-origin-of-marketing-vegas-what-happens-in
-vegas-stays-in-vegas on August 31, 2021.

McGonigal, J. (2010). *Gaming can make a better world* [Video file]. Accessed at www.ted.com/talks/jane_mcgonigal_gaming_can_make_a_better_world on August 12, 2021.

Mineo, L. (2021, June 3). *Racial wealth gap may be a key to other inequities.* Accessed at https://news.harvard.edu/gazette/story/2021/06/racial-wealth-gap-may-be-a-key-to-other-inequities on January 4, 2022.

Mississippi Department of Education. (2009). *Webb's Depth of Knowledge guide.* Accessed at www.aps.edu/sapr/documents/resources/Webbs_DOK_Guide.pdf on August 12, 2021.

Morrison, S., & Free, K. W. (2001). Writing multiple-choice test items that promote and measure critical thinking. *Journal of Nursing Education, 40*(1), 17–24.

Niguidula, D. (2019). *Demonstrating student mastery with digital badges and portfolios.* Alexandria, VA: Association for Supervision and Curriculum Development.

Ogle, D. (1986). K-W-L: A teaching model that develops active reading of expository text. *The Reading Teacher, 39*(6), 564–570.

Painter, J. (2004, September). *Writing and reviewing assessment items: Guidelines and tips.* Accessed at http://citeseerx.ist.psu.edu/viewdoc/download?doi=10.1.1.495.2874&rep=rep1&type=pdf on October 6, 2021.

Paris, S. G., Wasik, B. A., & Turner, J. C. (1991). The development of strategies of readers. In R. Barr, M. Kamil, P. Mosenthal, & P. D. Pearson (Eds.), *Handbook of reading research* (Vol. 2, pp. 609–640). Mahwah, NJ: Lawrence Erlbaum Associates.

Perkins, D. (2020, January 10). *Using the QFT to drive inquiry in project-based learning.* Accessed at www.teachthought.com/technology/using-the-qft-to-drive-inquiry-in-project-based-learning on August, 2021.

Peters, S. J., Carter, J., & Plucker, J. A. (2020). Rethinking how we identify "gifted" students. *Phi Delta Kappan, 102*(4), 8–13.

Peters, S. J., Rambo-Hernandez, K., Makel, M., Matthews, M., & Plucker, J. (2019). Effect of local norms on racial and ethnic representation in gifted education. *AERA Open*, 5(2), 1–18. Accessed at https://journals.sagepub.com/doi/full/10.1177/2332858419848446 on January 7, 2022.

Phillips, M. (2019, December 21). *How to hook your students instantly: The anticipatory set.* Accessed at https://completeliterature.com/how-to-hook-your-students-instantly-the-anticipatory-set on September 23, 2021.

Powell, W., & Kusuma-Powell, O. (2011). *How to teach now: Five keys to personalized learning in the global classroom.* Alexandria, VA: Association for Supervision and Curriculum Development.

Priest, N. (2016). *Digital badging and micro-credentialing.* Accessed at https://bostonbeyond.org/wp-content/uploads/2020/04/Digital_Badging_Paper_NMEF.pdf on August 12, 2021.

Reis, S. M., & Renzulli, J. S. (n.d.). *Curriculum compacting: A systematic procedure for modifying the curriculum for above average ability students.* Accessed at https://gifted.uconn.edu/schoolwide-enrichment-model/curriculum_compacting on September 15, 2021.

Reis, S. M., Renzulli, J. S., & Burns, D. E. (2016). *Curriculum compacting: A guide to differentiating curriculum and instruction through enrichment and acceleration* (2nd ed.). New York: Routledge.

Renzulli, J. S., & Reis, S. M. (2014). *The Schoolwide Enrichment Model: A how-to guide for talent development* (3rd ed.). Waco, TX: Prufrock Press.

Renzulli, J. S., & Smith, L. (1979). *A guidebook for developing individualized educational programs (IEP) for gifted and talented students.* Storrs, CT: Creative Learning Press.

Rogers-Whitehead, C. (2021, April 12). *How 3 gaming industry trends can boost education.* Accessed at www.iste.org/explore/tools-devices-and-apps/how-3-gaming-industry-trends-can-boost-education on December 20, 2021.

Rothstein, D., & Santana, L. (2017). *Make just one change: Teach students to ask their own questions.* Cambridge, MA: Harvard Education Press.

Sherrington, T. (2019). Teacher-led instruction and student-centred learning are opposites. In C. Barton & T. Bennett (Eds.), *The researchED guide to education myths: An evidence-informed guide for teachers* (pp. 71–82). Melton, Woodbridge, United Kingdom: John Catt Educational.

Smiderle, R., Rigo, S. J., Marques, L. B., Coelho, J. A. P. D., Jaques, P. A. (2020). *The impact of gamification on students' learning, engagement and behavior based on their personality traits.* Accessed at https://slejournal.springeropen.com/articles/10.1186/s40561-019-0098-x on January 6, 2022.

Smith, A. (2021). *9 lesson hook strategies to launch learning.* Accessed at www.teachstarter.com/us/blog/lesson-hook-strategies-to-launch-learning/ on January 6, 2022.

Sparks, S. D. (2017, May 16). *Children must be taught to collaborate, studies say.* Accessed at www.edweek.org/leadership/children-must-be-taught-to-collaborate-studies-say/2017/05 on January 5, 2022.

Spiller, J., & Butler, B. (2020). *Does "all" mean "all"? Labels, be gone!* Accessed at www.allthingsplc.info/blog/view/409/does-all-mean-all-labels-be-gone on August 12, 2021.

Takeuchi, L. M., & Vaala, S. (2014). *Level up learning: A national survey on teaching with digital games.* New York: The Joan Ganz Cooney Center at Sesame Workshop. Accessed at www.joanganzcooneycenter.org/wp-content/uploads/2014/10/jgcc_leveluplearning_final.pdf on January 6, 2022.

Terada, Y. (2019, March 14). *The science of drawing and memory: Want students to remember something? Have them draw it.* Accessed at www.edutopia.org/article/science-drawing-and-memory on September 23, 2021.

Terada, Y., & Merrill, S. (2020). *The 10 most significant education studies of 2020.* Accessed at www.edutopia.org/article/10-most-significant-education-studies-2020 on August 12, 2021.

Tom Schimmer Podcast. (July 25, 2021). *Yvette Jackson interview (episode 32—Tom Schimmer podcast)* [Video file]. Accessed at www.youtube.com/watch?v=yaFr54x7EKk on August 11, 2021.

Tucker, C. (2016, April 12). *Design your own digital choice board.* Accessed at https://catlintucker.com/2016/04/design-your-own-digital-choice-board/ on August 12, 2021.

United States Department of Education. (n.d.). *About IDEA.* Accessed at https://sites.ed.gov/idea/about -idea/ on August 11, 2021.

University of Michigan School of Information. (n.d.). *Digital game use: Teachers in the classroom.* Accessed at http://gamesandlearning.umich.edu/a-games/key-findings/survey-report/digital-game-use/ on August 11, 2021.

Usen, T. H. (1993). *The effects of pre-reading activities on reading comprehension.* [Doctoral dissertation, Kean College]. ERIC Institute of Education Sciences: https://files.eric.ed.gov/fulltext/ED355498.pdf

Warner, J. (2016, August 21). *I want to make students uncomfortable.* Accessed at www.insidehighered.com/blogs/just-visiting/i-want-make-students-uncomfortable on January 4, 2022.

Watanabe-Crockett, L. (2014). *The differences between projects and project-based learning.* Accessed at https://globaldigitalcitizen.org/the-differences-between-projects-and-projectbased-learning on August 12, 2021.

Webb, N. L. (2002). *Depth-of-knowledge levels for four content areas.* Accessed at https://apps.web.maine.gov/doe/sites/maine.gov.doe/files/inline-files/dok.pdf on September 16, 2021.

Webb, N. L. (2009). *Webb's Depth of Knowledge guide: Career and technical education definitions.* Accessed at www.aps.edu/sapr/documents/resources/Webbs_DOK_Guide.pdf on January 5, 2022.

Weichel, M., McCann, B., & Williams, T. (2018). *When they already know it: How to extend and personalize student learning in a PLC at Work.* Bloomington, IN: Solution Tree Press.

Westside Personalized. (2018, June). *A conversation with Michael Matera, author of "Explore like a pirate" (ep. 65)* [Audio podcast]. Accessed at https://podcasts.apple.com/us/podcast/conversation-michael-matera-author-explore-like-pirate/id1328946316?i=1000437633612&l=es on August 12, 2021.

Wiggins, G., & McTighe, J. (1998). *Understanding by design* (1st ed.). Alexandria, VA: Association for Supervision and Curriculum Development.

Willard-Holt, C. (2003, October). Raising expectations for the gifted. *Educational Leadership, 61*(2), 72–75.

Yoon, S. Y., & Gentry, M. (2009). *Racial and ethnic representation in gifted programs: Current status of and implications for gifted Asian American students.* Accessed at https://journals.sagepub.com/doi/pdf/10.1177/0016986208330564 on January 4, 2022.

Young, D. F. (2003). *The effects of instruction in prereading strategies on reading comprehension.* Accessed at https://soar.suny.edu/handle/20.500.12648/5518?show=full on March 1, 2022.

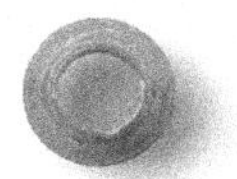

INDEX

D

F

G

H

I

J

K

L

M

N

O

P

Q

R

S

T

U

V

W

When They Already Know It
Mark Weichel, Blane McCann, and Tami Williams
Help your collaborative team address the question "How will we extend the learning for students who are already proficient?" The authors identify five elements of personalized learning and five instructional strategies for extending learning that give students the opportunity to reach their personal best.
BKF809

Enriching the Learning
Michael Roberts
Rely on *Enriching the Learning* to help your school community address question 4 of the Professional Learning Communities at Work® process. The book's wide range of strategies, templates, and tools is designed to fully prepare collaborative teams to plan and execute engaging extensions for students who have already demonstrated proficiency.
BKF889

You Can Learn!
Tim Brown and William M. Ferriter
Great learning starts when students believe in their academic abilities. In *You Can Learn!*, authors Tim Brown and William M. Ferriter introduce intentional and purposeful steps your PLC team can take to increase the self-efficacy of every learner.
BKG020

Unpacking the Competency-Based Classroom
Jonathan G. Vander Els and Brian M. Stack
Explore a variety of perspectives and examples from educators who have shifted to CBE with great results. The book details how to do the work by reevaluating and revamping traditional policies, structures, and procedures, including assessment and instruction practices.
BKG018

Visit SolutionTree.com or call 800.733.6786 to order.